1

Branded for Life

A true story of child abuse, rescue and murder

Det. Rick Meadows *with* Helen Phillips

Branded For Life

A true story of child abuse, rescue, and murder.

Co-Authored by:

Det. Rick Meadows and Helen Phillips

Copyright 2023

ISBN 979-8-9880775-0-3, 979-8-9880775-1-0, 979-8-9880775-2-7

www.brandedforlife.net

Contact: BrandedForLifeBook@gmail.com

Preface

I am a retired Law Enforcement Officer with 24 years and 8 months of service. I spent the last several years of my career working in the Crimes Against Children unit. These cases involved children, mostly under 12 years of age, who were victims of physical or sexual abuse and sometimes murder. I quickly learned the sadistic details of brutality, victimization and sexual deviation adults are capable of inflicting upon children. I was assigned the worst of the worst cases.

While there are numerous stories that I could share, this case was extraordinary and personal. I remained in contact with Shantay years after she was rescued from the most brutal torture and inhumane conditions I have witnessed. I attended special events such as her junior high and high school graduations. She knew I was committed to her and believing she could rise above her past. As you will learn from page one, Shantay valiantly fought to overcome the terrors of her childhood only to fall victim to the cycle of domestic violence that often snares survivors and repeats itself. In the midst of studying to become a counselor with dreams of working with troubled youth she was brutally murdered by her estranged boyfriend.

However, this book is not just about Shantay, it is also about me. How my childhood and my life prepared me to go into this work and come out fairly normal. This line of work takes its toll on those who do it. Seeing things that you cannot even talk about to friends or family builds up and the stress and trauma causes many to turn to alcohol, drug abuse, divorce etc. I cannot say that I have not suffered from PTSD, but I was lucky enough to have a support system that understands the gravity I felt. We want to let others who work these cases know that we understand. We offer a list of resources for victims of child abuse and those who suffer from working these cases on our website www.brandedforlife.net.

Why write a book with such a tragic ending? Why would anyone read it?

As Shantay grew from a child to a young adult, we discussed her desire to share her story. I encouraged her to write a book. We agreed that if one individual became more attentive and was aware that abuse crossed every economic, racial, social, and religious culture and is present in every neighborhood, classroom, and congregation, perhaps they would find the courage to report their concerns.

She wanted her story to empower the reluctant, knowing one call could save a child from another night of torture, violence, or rape. There were innumerable red flags; missed, discounted, or ignored. The scars and pleas of a desperate child unheeded. The systems mandated to intervene and protect repeatedly dropped the ball and she fell through the cracks. Her life and her death were a culmination of failures instead. My secondary goal is to inform. The courageous individuals who dedicate their lives to rescuing child victims suffer greatly as a consequence. Many times, I was asked "How do you do it? Are you OK?" My response was simply, I just do. Somebody must fight for the children, and I am OK. The truth is, I was not okay. Working these cases take their toll and cause emotional, mental, spiritual, and relational issues and repercussions that linger and ripple. Knowledge of and exposure to such horror is costly. Vicarious trauma is real. If you know someone working in this field, please make sure they have or get the support they need.

Shantay was denied the opportunity to write her story. With the help of Helen Phillips, this is my attempt to capture it for her. This is her story, our story from my perspective. "Branded for Life." I'm hoping she would somehow look at this attempt to tell her story and see not just the painful parts of her life but also the beauty that she brought into it and see the love with which she was redeemed. That she would not just appreciate those who helped and loved her, but that she as well as all children deserve that love. It is dedicated to the daughter she left behind the children who are suffering, and, to members of law enforcement who bear unseen scars from entering the battle to rescue the innocent.

NOTE: The facts and details are real. Names have been changed and some incidents have been scripted through creative license.

Rick Meadows

Acknowledgments

Rick would like to thank the following.

My wife, Becky for loving me and allowing me the time to work on this project.

I would like to thank my children, friends, and family who helped, reviewed, listened to ideas, and put up with my obsessions.

Thank you, Grandpa, and my parents for giving me the best childhood and a solid foundation to base my life, and for preparing me to face challenges that I never dreamed I would have to face.

Mike and Robin for your work, encouragement, and support. We wouldn't have made it without you.

Helen, you deserve so much credit. You have used your gifts to express my feelings, my memories and my goal. You got it. Without you this story would not be told. I am so grateful for your dedication and hard work. Even if I had a gift for words, I am sure I could not find the words to thank you enough for your efforts.

~

Helen would like to acknowledge and thank the following individuals.

Grace, for introducing me to Rick, and believing I could help him tell the story.

First responders whose lives are spent running into harm's way. I glanced behind the curtain, and no words can adequately honor your sacrifices.

Mark and Bethany, for sanctuary in between 'where I used to be and this reckoning.'

Dorothy Shelton, for carrying me in prayer through this transition.

Amy McKinney, for reviewing the manuscript in advance and providing invaluable feedback.

The brave little girl who cried in the dark. Thank you for trusting the detective who came to rescue you. You and your sister are not forgotten; your courage is as convicting as it is inspiring. I cannot wait to meet you on a distant shore.

Rick, for trusting me with something so personal. Thank you for allowing me to dig deeper; to get to know the man behind the badge. You handed me the threads and offered grace as I wove them together. This has been the honor of a lifetime. May it work justice and bring a measure of healing.

Most importantly, Jesus, for a lifetime of rescues. Thank you for drawing me into the wilderness, stripping my life bare, and pressing in until I understood it was time. This is for you and because of your life in me. May others find a way to turn from their personal darkness, and towards the light and find their redeemer.

CHAPTER 1

The world does not pause to grieve with us, nor do we with them. I suppose if all humanity grieved simultaneously, we would cease to exist.

CHAPTER 2

Waves of dread crashed over me as the funeral home came into view. Storm clouds shrouded the final remnants of blue sky with an oppressive gloom. A chill crept up my spine like fingers moving across a keyboard. Physically exhausted, and arrested by the weightiness of the moment, I felt trapped by a reality I could not escape. This cannot be how her story ends.

The timing of the memorial service coincided with pre-scheduled leave from work. I was grateful to retreat to the sanctuary of my home for the week preceding and following Shantay's memorial service. Preparations for the upcoming holiday were hijacked by the devastating and emotionally disruptive news of her murder. My mind had been seized by the unfolding details. I was spiraling downward reliving her child abuse case thirteen years prior. Shantay's life, and now her death, had interfused my professional and personal life as no other victim had.

The lengthy drive from home into town was deafeningly quiet, my soul fraught with melancholy. A melancholy so dark and suffocating it felt like my soul had slipped below the surface of quicksand. No lighthearted conversation with my wife Becky. No music filling the silence. I chose the scenic route in a vain attempt to delay our arrival. The countryside was dull and the barren trees a grayish brown. This stretch of winding road is a favorite of mine, especially driving in my restored Chevelle. The curves returned me to my high school years and the youthful anticipation of driving through the countryside to visit Becky.

Instead of being captivated by sweet remembrances, I was gripped by nostalgia. A familiar reluctance triggered memories of traveling to my grandpa's funeral when I was thirteen. My parents were in the front seat. My dad's strong, leathered hands firmly gripping two and ten on the steering wheel. My younger brother was beside me in the back

10

seat wearing his Sunday best. The only sound from the old Pontiac rambling down the back roads in Covington was the A.M. radio. The windows were rolled down and the air was blowing freely. Mom's hair was pulled back with a scarf. I thought it looked elegant, but I also thought she was prettier than other ladies at church. She dabbed her eyes with a hankie trying to be brave and catch her tears before they fell. Dad was the breadwinner, but mom was the rock that kept the family together. She rarely cried in front of me and my brother, and it was unnerving to see her upset. I did not know what to say or how to help.

My vision blurred from tears welling. I could feel a sob building in my gut and rising to my throat. I feared if the sound escaped it would frighten me and begin an avalanche of emotion that would consume our family right then and there.

I leaned my head slightly outside the window. I closed my eyes and felt the air rushing across my face. I held my breath and swallowed. "Grandpa, what am I going to do without you?"

It was my first great loss, and I felt tossed between sorrow and gratitude. So many of my best childhood memories include my grandpa. I could not imagine a future without that quiet thinker, a giant of a man in my eyes. Grandpa's absence left an irreplaceable void. Everything certain shifted and felt a bit unstable. For two young boys who had grown up fearlessly exploring the outdoors and known only the love and safety of our family, the impermanence of life had invaded our innocence. The childhood perception of invincibility shifted to one of appreciation and gratitude for the preciousness of life. Perhaps this was the moment the seeds sown in our earliest years took root, leading me and my brother toward careers in public service.

We had a special bond, and his gentle wisdom is the still small voice in my head. His face is not as clear, but his impact never diminished.

11

I wanted to honor his life by exemplifying it. I have been told I am a lot like him which is a tremendous honor. I can only hope it is true.

Shantay's death was a different loss, but similarly disruptive. I felt lost again and unsure how to navigate all that was stirring in the wake.

Becky noticed my far away eyes and asked, "are you okay," pulling me back to the present. I glanced at her soft blue eyes and responded with a nod. I was thinking about my grandpa.

I gazed upon the gently rolling hills and wooden fences neatly framing the boundaries between farms. Just as we crested the hill, dense cumulus clouds had parted, and brilliant rays of sunlight lit the horizon. As if heaven were reminding me that hope would find a way, just as it had when grandpa passed.

As we reached the edge of town the traffic was heavier. The suburbs were spreading further west encroaching upon the edges of the county. Investors were purchasing large swaths of land for development in hopes of drawing would-be residents from the city. The holiday season was in full swing. Homes and businesses were already adorned with Christmas themed décor.

As we stopped at a red light, I scanned the strip mall, the original anchor for chain restaurants, a gas station and drug store. On the adjacent corner was a sprawling new grocery store. Both parking lots were jammed with people flitting about so festive and carefree. A group of ladies engrossed in conversation were entering a coffee shop. Several men in rival team jerseys were walking toward the sports bar to enjoy the camaraderie of beer and football. As is often the case for someone suffering a loss or those repeatedly exposed to the dark side of humanity, a peculiar sense of betrayal turned to annoyance. My overreaction was irrational, and I felt flush with embarrassment. The warm remembrance of my grandpa and the comfort it brought were gone.

My apprehension for memorial services had increased over the years. Entering a hushed crowded room, and people segregated in clusters. The fragrance of lilies. Filing past the gloomy flower arrangements. But the worst by far is the well-intended mourner offering the bereaved some trite platitude about their loss being heaven's gain, or God needing another angel.

When death invades like a thief in the night, we are never prepared. Those who reason that death is inevitable, a natural process in the cycle of life, will one day feel the contradiction between reason and reality. Those who trust in science and lean on the laurels of modern medicine will find neither brings consolation at the graveside. Even those who trust in religion or eternal life may be alarmed when their faith wavers. The accusing echo of unanswered prayers have caused many to question God. Every tragedy, no matter what we believe, leaves people staggering. The fragility of life and our shared humanity cannot be denied. I have noted that every person that grieves, whether they are pushing through or being stoic, is deep down dealing with these complex emotions and doubts.

Walking through the valley of the shadow of death is an emotionally taxing journey we walk alone. This is especially true when the loss is a child or a young person. Loss is deeply personal and the grief we experience as unique as the person now missing from our stories. Death changes us… In its desolation we are expected to return to a life cruelly interrupted and into a future we did not choose. We walk in a paradox between the cherished memories of our loved one and reluctantly accepting life without them. We may find ourselves angry when we are finally able to laugh again, and impatient when those around us worry over trivial matters.

The world may pause with us momentarily, but life goes on. While the phrase feels heartless and accusatory if we're honest, once we catch our breath, how grateful we are that it does. How else would we carry on?

As author Simone Well so aptly stated, "There are only two things that pierce the heart: beauty and affliction. Moments we wish would last forever and moments we wish had never begun. How are we to interpret what they are saying?" The purest interpretation is to know we are made for more than what we see. There are questions that will remain unanswered. Death is an unavoidable pain written into the human narrative; but it is not the end of the story. Eventually we find new paths and recreate our lives. We acknowledge the emptiness then find the courage to honor their life by not allowing death to have the final say.

CHAPTER 3

Shantay's death had been a gut punch, and the savage nature of it hit like a bullet to the chest. Even when I caught my breath, I felt disoriented, and emotionally bruised. Yes, I had been given a privileged front row seat to her miraculous redemption. But I was also part of a small cadre of people familiar with her back story and the childhood abuse she barely escaped.

Watching the recap of Shantay's murder on local news was unnerving. The brutal details were being scattered like fodder across the airwaves. Photos of her ex-boyfriend were shown, and citizens were asked to contact law enforcement with any information regarding the crime or his whereabouts.

Domestic violence advocates had harnessed the public outcry to draw needed attention and community awareness. Alarming statistics confirmed that increasingly younger women were becoming trapped in the vicious cycle of domestic violence; some as early as middle school age.

In a surge of compassion and solidarity, the community had collectively gasped in devastation, reeled in heartbreak, and exhaled in mourning. Family, friends, neighbors and co-workers of Shantay and her mother Michaela, grieved together during a candlelight vigil. An array of flowers, balloons and candles began filling the courtyard of her apartment building. The benevolence of many brought little consolation to Michaela when nothing changed the reality she was forced to accept. Her baby girl was gone and the cowardice bully who took her life had absconded.

Slowly the media frenzy subsided and gave way to other breaking news. Ravenous reporters hunting for a soundbite of unscripted grief, had ceased camping out. Yet again the void of concern regarding the victims and their families returned.

The family's despair coupled with my own was punishing. Moments of preoccupation at work increased. When I found myself distracted, I would step away from my computer and take a lap around the building, until I could concentrate again. Trudging through workday tasks became challenging. The laid-back, engaged guy my co-workers were accustomed to had become withdrawn. As apathy for everyday concerns that felt meaningless creeped in, irritability began seeping out as curt responses to unwitting bystanders.

~

I had moved on from my role as a detective several years prior and was now using my skills in private industry. Increased pay, less predator chasing and no more immersion in violence against children, was a win-win. My wife celebrated my new freedom as well. Retirement had been within reach when a head-hunter pursued me with an extraordinary opportunity to move in a new direction. With less than six months from twenty-five years of service, I opted for early retirement, grabbed my shot, and got out.

Former co-workers from the police department and social services who were familiar with my long-term connection with Shantay had reached out. I selectively responded to voice mails and text messages. Their shock added to the fray. The confluence of facts, past, present, and surfacing were overwhelming. I was too close to the situation to neatly compartmentalize the mixture of emotions. I tried every method of professional detachment I had learned during my years in law enforcement, to no avail.

It was worse in the still of night. I found myself swept away in the tidal wave of images, emotions, and reminders. My willpower was no match for the intrusive ruminations.

The memories of her case had been buried in the collective storehouse of my mind with every other case I worked. A pandora's box had been exhumed and pried open. Even rest could not abate the onslaught. As if it were yesterday, I was back to the day I met Shantay thirteen years ago. All the events surrounding that introduction flooded back. I remembered sitting across from her in the guidance counselor's office. I had been called to investigate concerns of child abuse. Her arm swollen and bruised; her frail body swallowed by multiple layers of stained clothing. The stories that unfolded became one of the worst cases of child abuse I had seen.

~

Joining a specialty taskforce was a tremendous honor and advancement in my career. As a member of the Crimes Against Children Unit, I became part of an elite team and part of multiple covert operations. What no one can adequately describe beforehand is how any notion that humans are inherently good will erode. In a few intense years, a mural of children's faces, crime scenes, testimonies and disappointing outcomes had become part of my life's story. Rarely was a lasting connection forged with the child or their family.

The last three years of my law enforcement career catapulted me down a dark and formidable path into child exploitation. I was honored by the promotion to detective, welcoming the transition. My soul was exposed to the depths of immorality; a licentious underworld where reprobates and lewd predators roamed free. I had known only shadows of such abominations.

Becky noticed a slow, progressive shift in my disposition. I became suspicious and hyper vigilant about who our children spent time with. Cynicism and mistrust trickled through in comments and reactions. She was concerned and supported me as best she could. Even as my intimate companion, and the one who knows me better than I know myself, she was naïve, and I would take it to my grave before sullying her virtue.

Even now, with law enforcement fifteen years in the rearview mirror, if I allow my thoughts to wander, a mural of tear-stained faces, twisted with grief, can ambush me. The beautiful young woman we would soon be saying farewell to, was one of those cases.

~

As we approached the funeral home, I slowed the car and waited my turn. A procession of mourners streamed from every direction, the line wrapping around the building. Before we exited the car, I paused to collect myself. Breathing in deeply and exhaling slowly. Becky reached for my hand and squeezed gently. "I love you." Her soft voice calmed many storms in my life. I wanted to acknowledge I had been distracted and not myself and admit I had been cross. But she knew all that, and accepted the only words I offered, "I'm glad you are here with me. Love ya Beck."

As we joined those filing into the funeral home, I felt no more prepared to say goodbye than the moment I learned she was gone. Today would bring no closure. Her murderer was still at large. The only thread of consolation was the hope for justice that eluded her in the past.

I asked grandpa for strength. I could not bear to see Shantay's lifeless body. I have seen my share of postmortem bodies. I have participated in the autopsies of children. My familiarity with the deceased was subverting my ability to detach, one of the best weapons I had against personalization of the hurt. Such intimate knowledge and experience amplified my grief process. This crime was personal.

CHAPTER 4

In the years that followed working Shantay's case, I maintained contact with her and her new family. Witnessing the progressive transformation of her life was a rare gift. After her second adoption I was an honored guest at various celebrations. The joyful refrain of these moments was deeply gratifying. I mailed Christmas and birthday gifts until she reached high school age. Every handwritten thank-you note served as a reminder of how far she had come. Even watching her penmanship improve made me smile.

Her confidence blossomed as untapped potential met a garden of opportunity. When her personality was no longer repressed, an energetic, playful, and humorous nature emerged. I was honored to witness her life being restored. The once shy and despondent little girl had grown into a poised, fun-loving, and academically strong teenager. This was the outcome we desired for every child. Sadly, endings this extraordinary are infrequent.

Michaela had taken in foster children for many years. She was a passionate and deeply religious woman, who desired to provide refuge for as many children as she could. But when the time came for the children to move on, saying goodbye became increasingly more difficult. She longed to become a permanent solution, a home where children never had to leave. Shantay had been the second of two girls she formally adopted.

On her first birthday with Michaela, Shantay was surrounded by the love and affection of many, including me. As we belted out a chorus of "Happy Birthday to You," in disjointed harmony, Michaela presented her with a beautiful two-tiered cake. A flavorful work of art covered with white swirls, scalloped edges, and pink flowers. Flickering candles encircled her name written in pink cursive. "Make a wish and blow them out, sweet girl," her mother told her. Joy radiated from her once weary countenance. It was a snapshot of bliss watching her savor her first taste of positive, undivided attention. "This is the prettiest cake I have ever seen," she said and then blew out eleven candles with one breath.

Her new mom was an exceptional person and she had truly found her way home. If I had not been privy to the details of her ravaged childhood, I would not have believed it was the same child. The trauma of pervasive and severe childhood abuse would always threaten to creep back in. Truth seemed to triumph, but it was a far too rare moment of success. After more than a decade, no one could deny how dramatically light had overcome the darkness.

Yet, despite our best efforts, areas of unhealed trauma, deeply rooted lies, and the longing to be loved by a man created pathways for victimization to return. This time it demanded final say. It all felt so cruel.

Her purity was desecrated during infancy. Before her earliest memory, her psyche had been dominated by abuse and complex trauma. Relentless victimization sabotaged every domain of childhood development. Deprived of healthy attachments with caregivers, her ability to trust, and manage stressful emotions, had been impaired. Warped beliefs about self and others were deeply ingrained. The consequences of adverse childhood trauma were compounded by years of encountering adults who could have intervened but did not. Physical wounds were publicizing the narrative of her home life. Yet even the portrait engraved on her body, and other somatic complaints, were ignored. Pain was normalized.

Some might argue that statistically returning to the familiarity of abuse was inevitable, even multiplied by the extended delayed intervention. If that is true, then every person who did not intervene shares in the culpability. To those in the trenches working on their cases, these children are far more than stats. Every one of them deserves that we not pre-determine their likelihood of success. Counseling should be mandatory and include the provision of skills and resources to work through and overcome their past as a lifelong journey. Her history did not have to limit her potential or pre-determine her future.

Society is more aware of the lingering symptoms of childhood trauma, such as post-traumatic stress disorder, but much more is needed. Mental health agencies, school personnel, first responders, students, parents, and churches must be better equipped to recognize the signs and symptoms and seek help for themselves and others.

~

After a few tumultuous years with an abusive boyfriend, Kevin, who she met in college, Shantay became pregnant. She returned from out of state and Michaela had rejoiced over answered prayers, although she was not pleased that her daughter was pregnant. The courage to start over came too late. Her hopes and dreams were stolen when her estranged boyfriend unleashed hellish fury upon her in a final act of cowardice. Investigators concluded that a physical assault escalated into blind rage until he took her life. Shantay had old bruises and fresh defensive wounds on her hands.

Kevin had recently been arrested for banging her head against the wall and strangling her to the point of unconsciousness. The restraining order she filed six weeks prior to the murder stated Kevin had threatened to kill her. It was not a power-play after a lover's tryst, she was truly in fear for her life. But he was shrewd, twisting the truth to guilt her into relenting. Under the guise of needing her help, he began harassing her relentlessly claiming she was the reason he had no place to stay. He had manipulated and provoked her until she conceded and gave him refuge in her home. Her phone later revealed a barrage of calls and text messages from every angle of persuasion.

Now Michaela was enduring the greatest agony a human can suffer, the loss of her beloved daughter. Compounding her grief was how grisly her life ended; in excruciating pain and abandoned to die alone. Michaela is one of the strongest women I know, taking in and nurturing foster children in crisis. Overcoming such a devastating and senseless loss seemed unfathomable.

Thankfully, the court granted Michaela immediate, temporary custody of Shantay's daughter, Anna. It brought a measure of consolation, but grief, loss and regret would echo for years. Focusing on the child, the perfect likeness of her momma, would keep her from drowning in mourning. She would raise her granddaughter keenly aware that one day Anna may learn the morbid details of her mother's death. Michaela had done everything she could to shield her, but she could not undo the truth.

CHAPTER 5

Michaela and I spoke not long after Shantay's murder. She was feeling torn between two worlds; life before her daughter's murder and an unknown future, and was trapped in a holding pattern, unable to finalize Shantay's memorial service until her body was released by the medical examiner. She was living every mother's nightmare. Sleep eluded her and grief invaded every waking moment. Weeks had passed since the murder and Kevin was still a fugitive; the manhunt spread to multiple states.

I learned bits and pieces about the weeks and days preceding Shantay's murder from a variety of sources. News reports, family and friends of the family, and a few connections close to the investigation. I was relieved to learn that the night before the murder, Shantay's daughter, Anna, was at a sleepover with Michaela, who she affectionately called Gigi. Michaela kept the toddler for special Gigi time while affording Shantay time to focus on schoolwork, as well as enjoy a well-deserved gift of self-care in the form of a pedicure and a morning to sleep in. No plans had been made for a time to return Anna to Shantay.

Shantay had recently enrolled in classes at a local community college, determined to obtain her degree. She had lost ground academically and diligent study was required to catch up. Most of her courses had transferred, and with the help of the admissions counselor, she formulated a plan and adjusted the timeline to complete her courses. They had even discussed several avenues for internships to evaluate the best match for her strengths and interests.

Michaela delighted in spending time with Anna and their bond had grown quickly. When Shantay moved closer and distanced herself from Kevin, she welcomed her mother into a nurturing role in Anna's life. The only thing that rivaled Michaela's joy of being a new "Gigi" was watching Shantay engage as a mom.

Shantay's apartment in the city was on a month-to-month lease. When Kevin moved into her apartment, he showed no interest in spending time with Shantay's family. His decision was likely fueled by his increased lack of control and short fused aggressive behavior toward her. When Kevin was around, Shantay withdrew and remained distant from her family. Shantay had confided in friends that almost immediately after he moved in, they were fighting and it rapidly escalated. Many details were not revealed until after her death, when it was too late for those who loved her to intervene. He moved to Virginia with the primary goal of vengeance.

After Shantay filed a restraining order against Kevin and fled the city, Michaela offered to cosign a lease for an apartment on the condition that Kevin would not be allowed inside the premises. Shantay found one close to her mom and other family members and seemed to be enjoying a renewed sense of independence.

Shantay settled into her new apartment and quickly established a routine for Anna. A small 'welcome home' celebration was hosted and friends from Michaela's church and extended family lavished her with groceries and household items. A few ladies gathered around Shantay and Anna before they left and prayed for their protection. Shantay tried her best to harness the winds of change. With a few gift cards, she transformed her sterile apartment into a lovely home for her and Anna. Those closest to her breathed a sigh of relief.

Shantay wrestled with denying Kevin access to Anna and admitted to friends it would infuriate him. Friends suspected it was a ploy to keep his claws in her, but she was convinced a compromise benefited Anna. She tried to establish boundaries, insisting Kevin schedule visits with Anna in advance, insisting they only meet in public places like a park. When Kevin realized Shantay would always bring a friend, he stopped showing up.

There were tough conversations between mom and daughter about forgiveness, mutual respect, and what healthy boundaries looked like. Michaela was prepared to support her daughter, and Shantay promised to communicate more openly. An older friend of Shantay's, herself a survivor of domestic violence, recommended she find a counselor, but she resisted. Shantay confided her embarrassment that living with Kevin had failed again. She was guarded about disclosing details that would tarnish his reputation, which seemed worse in a circle of other survivors. She struggled with accepting she was a victim and not partly responsible for provoking him. While this is a typical trauma response for a co-dependent, domestic violence relationship, it was a clue that she was caught in the web of his lies. In contrast, she readily accepted the invitation from another friend to join a self-defense class and began practicing the techniques, never missing a class.

Grateful to be a family again, mom and daughter were hopeful about their restored but different relationship. Shantay would smile and shake her head watching Michaela with Anna, saying "You are going to spoil that girl, aren't you?" Shantay missed having a grandma until she was almost eleven. She wanted her daughter to have the things she had been denied.

Shantay's family encouraged her to rekindle previous friendships with classmates and her church family. Much of that never came to fruition. Perhaps she was imprisoned by fear of rejection or being judged. She purposefully avoided anyone she thought would chastise her for having sex outside of marriage. There were many who would have supported her, had they known her needs. Shantay seemed to focus on putting the past behind her, raising her daughter, and obtaining her degree. Her goal to work with at-risk youth had been solidified.

Michaela had no intention of leaving full-time work to raise a little one. But oh, how she loved every minute of being a "Gigi" and being a family again. Empty nesting, both adopted daughters living independently, she welcomed the opportunity to provide bucket loads of love and attention.

Michaela had taken the day off, giving herself a long weekend. She wanted Shantay to sleep in, but she was just as excited about enjoying unhurried time with Anna. The morning was spent leisurely, cooking Anna's favorite breakfast, pancakes with a fruit shaped smiley face, and bacon. Followed by cuddling on the couch and Michaela reading every book Anna selected, creating animated voices for the characters in each story. Shantay was almost eleven when she entered Michaela's life. The early formative years were past. Neither Michaela nor her daughters knew the simple pleasure of being captivated by story time.

When Anna said she missed her momma, Michaela attempted to text Shantay. After no response she called her cell, but it went to voice mail. Michaela had no reason for concern, but she shifted gears and moved toward taking Anna home. She helped Anna make her bed, got her dressed, and brushed her teeth. After dressing, she puttered in the kitchen, putting dinner in a crockpot and dishes in the dishwasher, then gathered Anna's things and repacked the special overnight bag they had picked out together. Before she left, Michaela called out to her mother, who lives with her, and she came down and kissed Anna goodbye.

The drive was short, and she wanted to avoid showing up unannounced. After Anna was secure in her car seat, she called again. No answer. They both agreed their history was tarnished by poor communication, and Michaela resisted assuming the worst. Learning to parent an adult child was strange and unfamiliar territory. Michaela's nurturing heart wanted to pull her close and protect them. Shantay asked for trust and space.

Michaela noticed Shantay's car in its assigned spot. She unfastened Anna from her car seat and gave her a squeeze before reaching for her overnight bag. It was the first sense that something was amiss. For a moment she wished she had left Anna at home, but quickly pushed away the fear. When she reached Shantay's apartment door, she realized the door was unlocked. Fear bristled the hair on her neck and goose bumps covered her arms. She entered to eerie silence. Shantay always had music playing or the TV on for background noise. She was not used to living alone and it was an adjustment. During the day, her mood was upbeat. She might be found singing and Anna dancing around her momma wearing dress-up clothes. Nighttime was different. A thick shroud of sadness would envelop her. Her anxiety soared to crippling, and she would struggle to see a way out. She would say the isolation was unbearable. She started calling Michaela and asking her to stay on the phone until she was sleepy. Sometimes talking distracted her, other times she asked Michaela to pray. Often no words were needed; they would watch the same TV show in silence.

Michaela began to call out Shantay's name. Then repeated herself. But there was no response. She walked to the living room, found the remote, turned to a children's program and sat Anna down on the couch. "Honey, I need you to stay right here on the couch, and do not move. Can you do that for me? I will be right back."

~

Michaela moved through the tiny kitchen/dining room nook. Everything seemed to be in place. Shantay was almost compulsive about maintaining order. It helped her feel in control when life felt out of control. It was a healthier coping mechanism than most. She called out to Shantay again and was met with silence. Michaela's heart was pounding. She moved up the stairs toward the bedroom almost in slow motion. As she ascended the steps, clinging to the railing, an indescribable smell filled her nostrils. She knew something horrible had happened and she should grab the baby and run for help. Her stomach twisted in knots and the smell made her gag.

As she reached the landing and slid past the washing machine protruding in the hallway, she could see the bedroom door was open and the smell was more pungent. Trembling, terrified, like a nightmare she could not awaken from, she leaned forward and peered around the door frame. There, motionless, was her daughter's body, lying on her right side, left hand reaching. She was surrounded by blood.

The psyche does bizarre things when reality is incomprehensible. Her mother's eyes stared at her daughter's delicate feet with freshly painted toenails. Their final conversation had been yesterday when Shantay left the nail salon. She thanked her mom for watching Anna and told her how much she loved her. Michaela began to scream, releasing a bloodcurdling wail. She collapsed to the floor beside her daughter. Her chest, neck and torso were covered in blood. There was so much blood. Her thin nightgown was torn and soaked through. Michaela's motherly instincts wanted to cover her. She fumbled to call 911 for help.

Unable to speak when she heard a voice on the other line, a terrifying guttural sound rose from her belly, so loud she could not hear the emergency operator's questions. Technology allowed emergency personnel to pinpoint their location, but they were unsure what had happened. Police and EMS were dispatched simultaneously. When Michaela finally gasped for air, she was barely cognizant of Anna's voice calling out from the bottom of the stairs, now terrified as well.

Before the police arrived, Michaela had stumbled down the stairs trying to prevent her granddaughter from seeing Shantay. She had scooped up the toddler and clung to her for dear life. Shouts from multiple police officers pierced her terrified stupor like lightening splits the sky. As officers entered the premises with weapons drawn

Michaela dropped to her knees grasping Anna so tightly it seemed to frighten the child. Michaela's hands had blood on them which smeared Anna's shirt when she picked her up. Her blood-soaked pants from kneeling beside Shantay had smeared the living room carpet. Initially no one was sure if either were hurt.

Amid the soul-crushing despair and hysteria, Michaela managed to convey between sobs, that her daughter had been murdered, her body was upstairs, she knew who killed her and that he was no longer in the premises. When firefighters arrived, they walked straight to Michaela and Anna, and began assessing them for injuries, asking her questions, checking her pulse, and taking her blood pressure. With every drop of compassion responders possessed, they attempted to calm the inconsolable mother. Her world collapsed around her and would never be the same. Shock is a merciful tonic, the mind protecting itself from snapping in two. But many moments of the events had been burned in her memory.

Grief poured out in the form of confusion, disbelief, regret, and anger as minutes ticked away. She would catch her breath and suddenly shout out loud, didn't anyone hear them fighting? How long was she lying there? How did he get into the apartment? Why didn't someone call the police? The questions were assailing her, and she verbalized them as quickly as they came. "My sweet girl was in love with a monster. My grandbaby's father is a murderous monster. I don't think I can survive this. He took her from us for no reason at all."

CHAPTER 6

"Rick, do you remember that first year she lived with me? It took a lot of patience, affection, and conversations before she fully integrated into the family. The rhythm of our days was consistent, and love was never withdrawn based on behavior. We built in flexibility and space to be spontaneous. We baked cookies, played in the leaves, and enjoyed family game night weekly. Those activities often led to family discussions, organically establishing secure attachment, and reinforcing that we were glad to be with them. We lived out our commitment like we had taken a vow before God. Shantay softened, became less guarded and more engaged. She began sharing how she felt, and we would explore why she was quiet or what happened that made her feel sad or powerless. Expanding her emotional vocabulary was so helpful. We worked on developing coping skills and how to self-regulate. This dispelled her anxiety sometimes. She was so resilient.

"Remember how her confidence soared when her grades improved. Even though she initially resisted my rule about reviewing her homework, she eventually understood the purpose. As her grades continued to improve, she began looking forward to our special time together. I realized much more than homework was being accomplished during these precious times together. She loved reading aloud, practicing spelling words, or working through the latest math concept her teacher had introduced. I relished in her desire to learn and the trust she began to demonstrate

"It was almost two years before she and Rochelle legally became my daughters. It will always be one of my happiest memories. Me, the girls, my mom, my aunt, and my dear friend Ruby, who became their surrogate grandmother, had a special ceremony at home before court. I promised to always love and take care of them. We gave them necklaces and flowers as a symbolic reminder. Later when the judge declared us a family, and the girls were given my name, we hooped and hollered, thanked God, cried tears of joy, and jumped up and down in a group hug. We did not care who was watching.

"The girls began to flourish beyond anything we could have imagined. Shantay and Rochelle shared a special bond too. I know it was different from the relationship Shantay had with her biological sister Anita. She missed Anita and nothing could fill that empty place. But Shantay and Rochelle picked on each other and became the best of friends in their own way. It was healing and belonging for both. They supported each other's dreams as they went separate directions after high school. I have since learned that Rochelle knew a few things about Kevin that Shantay had made her promise not to tell us.

"I will never forget how thrilled she was when you found a doctor willing to repair her ripped ear so she could wear earrings again. She could not imagine such kindness toward her. And when she was in high school you found an ophthalmologist willing to replace her damaged eye with an ocular implant. She told me later, that was the first time she felt pretty. What a difference that made! She was so proud when she posed for senior pictures, and there was no evidence of her damaged vision.

"She graduated with honors and earned a scholarship for college. It was truly miraculous. I was worried about her decision to attend college out of state. She had matured so much and felt ready to take on the world. But she wanted a boyfriend and did not agree with my rules about dating. It created tension and she was pulling away. It is a mother's job to give them roots and wings, so I supported her but reluctantly.

"Rick, he beat all the hope and light and life we worked so hard to rebuild. He tried to shatter her dreams and make her surrender them. His abuse slowly infiltrated their relationship. His fuse was short, and worse when he was drinking. He spewed demeaning words at her that eroded her confidence. I do not know how much he knew about her childhood abuse, but she was clearly triggered by his aggressiveness. She became self-conscious and insecure about her body. She shut down and became withdrawn. By the time she left him, she was a shadow of the confident young woman who left my home ready to conquer the world.

"Kevin's abuse escalated when they moved to the city. In the end, even the newly acquired self-defense skills were no match for his brutish outrage. Rick, I knew he was violent, but she had not told me everything. I had no idea how heinous his behavior had become. There had been several incidents in the past few months, but she only told each incident to a different friend. It was not until we put it all together that we fully understood. It was staggering.

"I do not think she would have left him if it were not for Anna. She became a protective lioness with her little girl. When his violence erupted in front of their daughter, she rallied that resilience she had as the young girl we knew. As blurred as those lines were for herself, she would never put her daughter through the hell of her childhood. Conviction burned and fueled the courage she needed to take a stand. She was humiliated and embarrassed. I was not sure how to restore her confidence, or how much time it would take for her to trust herself.

"Anna gave her something to focus on, someone to fight for, and a reason not to settle for survival. She was determined to be a good mom and prove her childhood had not stolen her chance for happiness.

"I know she begrudged the restrictions I imposed during her teen years. Did I push too hard? I followed my convictions and the wisdom of those around me. I was scared for her and unsure if she was equipped to make good choices when it came to boys. I did not want to control her, I wanted to protect her. I know what can happen when young girls get involved with guys too quickly and hormones take over.

"When she was eating well and rested, she faced life differently. She began leaning more into her faith. She would read scripture and discuss things she remembered from bible study and church. She found renewed grit, and I was hopeful. She had an audacious way of approaching God. She knew he was with her as a child and had answered her pleas. It gave her a boldness and tenacity that she had forgotten. Rick, you were part of why she believed God loved her. He brought you into her horror story and rescued her. She knew he had not forgotten her then or given up on her now. He would rescue her again.

"Anita's passing was a defining moment in her faith. It could have been the final blow that kept her from believing God was real. But she did not turn away. We had long conversations about why God allowed such terrible things to happen. She was confused and angry that her sister had died. She wondered how he could take the person she loved the most. She wrestled with God unafraid to be honest. She believed God could give her the strength to change for Anna. Laughter and effervescence hid a deep thinker who contemplated tough questions.

"She knew that if you had been the one who investigated her sister's case, she would not have been returned to the family. She also felt guilty that her sister suffered more than she had. I know it is twisted, but she believed the abuse she suffered connected her to her sister. At times, her musings seemed peculiar, but there was a purity and fearlessness in her dialogues with God. I admired her honesty. I know many a mature saint that has never faced their own 'demons' or dared to ask such provoking questions. She understood the Lord was the only one who truly knew her history. She believed he was an ally that never left her, even though she knew pain made her different from

33

others. When the heavens were silent and she was weary of trying to understand why so many others had loving homes and parents, she returned to one undeniable truth. God had not abandoned her. He brought you into her life to save her from the Hunters. To her that made you a hero. Rick, that is why she always introduced you to others that way. It was never just a compliment or flattery; it was her truth.

"Shantay hid the full extent of his abusive behavior from me. Some of that may have been denial. I do not know whether she was protecting him or afraid or both. School kept him busy and at arm's length for a while. He was using Anna to get to her. He would demand his rights and threaten to take her to court. He had no interest in the fiscal responsibility of being a dad, but he was a cunning manipulator. He would quickly shift his position when it served him and say he knew all about the other guys she slept with and that she had no proof Anna was his. Of course, that was not true. He might have been the only man she knew intimately. His words pierced her heart. His interest and attention vacillated. When he had a girlfriend, he did not care as much. When they saw what a jerk he was, he would turn back to her.

"During football season, Kevin's star athlete status made him popular, but arrogant and unbearable. She was troubled by rumors that he was unfaithful, but denied their validity until there were too many to ignore. I prayed he would move on. She may have been heartbroken for a while, but better off in the end. The pregnancy was unintentional, but she was convinced a baby would bring them together. He vocalized his resentment on social media. He openly ranted about not having a say in her decision to keep the baby and having to pay for a child he did not choose to have. The accolades from coaches and fans, including women vying for his attention was not enough.

"He did not play football in his senior year. His dreams of being drafted were off the table and he was lost without football. Then he discovered she was dating again. It was rare because she had Anna. But she might go to dinner with a friend of a friend. Somehow, Kevin caught wind of it, and was infuriated. He resented knowing she no longer pined for him.

"She confided to friends that he began harassing her, relentlessly and obsessively. Calling her constantly, texting, leaving extremely long messages when she did not answer. I suggested she block his number, but she felt she could not because of Anna. Then he began showing up at odd times on weekends, following her and learning her routine. He would make his presence known and then watch her from a distance. It made her feel vulnerable. When he had been drinking, he would interrupt whatever she was doing and cause a scene. It did not take long for him to spiral into irrational and overtly possessive behavior. She stopped going out. I thought it was because she was focused on schoolwork and Anna.

"She had reconnected with a few trusted friends she knew before college. She tried a support group for victims of domestic violence but admitted to a friend that she was uncomfortable betraying him. Talking about his actions made her feel guilty even as the behavior became more volatile and more frequent. She was conflicted and ashamed. Rick, she knew how I felt and closed me out. She believed they had a chance and would make it work, proving us wrong. Despite her growing fear of what he might be capable of, she clung to the fantasy that they would be a family. She kept her heart ajar for three years after getting pregnant."

CHAPTER 7

Becky wrapped her arm through mine as we passed through the vestibule. I felt suspended in time. The preceding days left me storm tossed. Thrashed between disbelief, fury, and sorrow, my heart was navigating grief on its own terms. As we approached the open doorways, muffled voices became more distinguishable. I was so thankful Becky was by my side. She was as lost for words as I had been with Michaela. Her presence was enough. Becky knew I remained in contact with Shantay and her family. She understood that we had forged a rare connection from the moment our lives intersected. I became emotionally invested and the loss felt deeply personal.

I signed the guest book and scanned the crowd. When I saw the closed casket, relief washed over me. I glanced at Becky who mirrored my relief. Overcome by empathy, she looked away to keep from crying.

Shantay's obituary affectionately described her as an easy-going, sometimes sassy, upbeat, social butterfly, with a cheerful outlook, and a smile that would light up the room. She was known for her love of music, and dance, home cooked meals, travel, animals and especially the company of friends and family. She was an accomplished college student with ambitions and a single mom to a precious daughter.

What it did not say is that Shantay was also a courageous survivor of the worst case of child abuse I had ever worked. Our connection began when she was a malnourished, frightened, severely verbally, physically, mentally, and emotionally abused child. Call it fate or coincidence, but I was at the right place, at the right time, with the proper training when the call came in. I led a team of investigators whose skill and dedication resulted in her liberation from a prison of torture at the hands of her adoptive parents. Unnerved by the sadistic irony of violence and abuse having boomeranged. It seemed as if the devil himself had skulked on the fringe of her life waiting to return and devour his prey. Her life had been a beautiful redemption story. Now it would never be completed.

It did not take long for Michaela to recognize me. She excused herself, turned and embraced me like an old friend. I understood her pain more profoundly than most. She held on with an overwhelming sense of mutual knowing and wept openly. I fought back the tears. When we finally made eye contact, language could not articulate the mutual grief. Emotion hung thick in the room. The only words that formed were, "Michaela, I am so sorry that she is gone. I'm so terribly sorry."

"I know, Rick. Me too. Thank you so much for being here. It means the world," she responded.

"Michaela, you gave her a brand-new life. She finally felt loved and worthy of love, and she flourished because of you. You were a great mom, and you gave her a good life." Michaela nodded as tears rolled faster than she could dab them with her tissue. "How are you doing?" I continued fumbling for words.

"Rick, I am inconsolable, outraged, and exhausted. I have not slept since that morning. Knowing he has not been captured is maddening. Detectives stay in touch, but they have no firm leads. The police believe he fled the state. The search began where he was raised but has extended to other states where family members live. They questioned his parents who said they had not seen or heard from him. I do not buy it. I know he is too selfish to attempt grabbing Anna, but I cannot let her out of sight. I avoid going out, and I look over my shoulder when I do. My coworkers have been supportive, donating leave and insisting I take as much as I need. And my church family, you know how loving they are. They keep bringing meals; my goodness I have never seen so much food and you know how my family loves to feast," she said with a soft chuckle.

"Yes, I certainly do," I replied. "Southern cooking at its finest."

"In my heart I know she is in heaven. She is free from pain and suffering. That is the only comfort. I miss her desperately. I want more time with her. I want her baby girl to know how special and amazing and beautiful her momma was. I had so much hope for her.

"Several people from the girl's high school were the first to show up when the news broke. Between phone calls, text messages and visitors, we have not had time to feel alone. Someone has insisted on staying every night even though my mom is there. The house has become a gathering place for more visitors than we have seen in ages. Stacks of cards fill the mailbox each day, their words filled with comfort and offers of support. So many flowers have been delivered. If only it were possible for my anguish to be extinguished by love. I feel prayers colliding with profound sadness, wrapping around me like a blanket against winter's chill. It is the only reason I have not lost my mind. Dozens of people have posted on her Facebook page, sharing memories and ways she touched their lives. And look at all these beautiful people who have gathered for my girl."

The line of mourners waiting to offer condolences had grown, but Michaela remained focused on our conversation. "There is someone I want you to meet," she said, gently turning me toward a loveseat in the corner. Sitting beside Michaela's mother Lori was a petite little girl. The child reminded me of another little girl I met so many years ago. Michaela bent down, opened her arms, and motioned for her to come. The little girl ran to her opened arms. Michaela scooped her up, squeezing her tightly and rocking her gently.

"This is Anna, Shantay's sweet baby girl."

"Anna, this is Detective Meadows," she said with her voice cracking. "He was your momma's hero." The little girl looked at me with radiant brown eyes and smiled softly. She waved her tiny hand and laid her head against Michaela shoulder.

No matter how often I asked either Michaela or Shantay not to preface their introductions that way, they insisted on doing so. With close family they would add, "he saved her life when she was a little girl." Hearing the words caused a lump to form in my throat. It was humbling and the attention made me uncomfortable.

~

When Michaela was granted permanent legal custody of her two foster daughters, she chose not to focus on the abuse they had endured. They lived as if their new beginning was filled with promise, potential and hope. In fact, Michaela denied herself access to full disclosure about Shantay's past. She refused to view her daughters as victims. She did not want to indulge or overcompensate; she wanted to establish healthy family dynamics. She believed she could love them into wholeness and focused every modicum of energy into positivity. It did not matter what anyone else thought, it worked for them, and her dedication paid off.

Michaela was not naïve about the residual effects of trauma or abuse; she simply chose not to center their lives on the past. She poured herself into helping the girls develop healthy coping skills and discovering constructive ways to channel and express emotion through art, sports, dance, and music. She lavished them with affection and created routines that brought stability and consistency into their lives. And she prayed fiercely. The transition into their new family was sprinkled with opportunities for the girls to have fun and be silly. A robust extended family and supportive church friends also doted on the girls. Michaela genuinely believed the girls would overcome their pasts without focusing on them. She devoted her life to creating an environment that reinforced her love and their value every day.

~

Michaela set Anna down, who then skipped back to Lori. Michaela and her mother had been actively involved in Anna's life since Shantay returned. They were Shantay's primary babysitters when she worked or needed a break from single parenting.

Michaela and I only spoke a few times over the last few years. Calls would come out of the blue, when she had something significant to share. I knew Shantay's history like no one else did, and she enjoyed reconnecting and updating me. Shantay had excelled in a private school and graduated with an advanced diploma and exceptional grades. A far cry from the learning disability classes forced upon her by her former adoptive mother.

After years of inseparability, Shantay and her mom reached the teenage years where the influence of peers was tremendous. They experienced a typical season of tension and conflict as she transitioned into the final years of high school. Turbulence rose when Shantay began challenging rules about dating and curfew. They butted heads on issues she felt were too strict. Michaela had not been concerned at the time, just frustrated about choices Shantay was making that did not align with the beliefs she had been taught.

Shantay's academic diligence granted her a scholarship from an out of state college. Her course work had been structured toward the goal of becoming a licensed clinical social worker. She loved every minute of it even though focusing became a challenge.

Her desire to find a boyfriend had become distracting. She wanted to experience affection and intimacy, but it was more than youthful curiosity. Away from family and friends, she seemed lost. Searching for belonging and surety in the eyes of a thousand strangers. Someone, anyone, where is home? The damage inflicted by early childhood abuse seemed to resurface and overshadow reason. She admitted never feeling "normal" but could never articulate why she felt different. Reoccurring memories of abuse began infiltrating her perception of situations and new friendships and spoke as if betrayal was inevitable. There was a cavernous void in her sense of identity, and success had not convinced her she was valued or worthy. Behind the laughter she was desperate for approval and validation and more vulnerable than anyone knew. Removed from accountability to her mother and cautionary wisdom of friends, she fell prey to charms of a charismatic, star athlete. She knew few examples of healthy male role models and not a father, uncle, brother or the like was watching over her. So, she settled for crumbs of attention, devoured them as if her survival depended on it.

She quickly discovered how moody her newly found infatuation could be. His inflated ego hid deep insecurity. When post-game attention waned, he acted petty and bullish behind closed doors. He was prone to sulking and jealousy. At first the abuse was subtle. His complements on her clothing and appearance became a source of wild accusations and derogatory comments. He became suspicious, questioning her whereabouts when she left or returned. It progressed to slander and verbal assaults insinuating she was being flirtatious or trying to draw the attention of other guys. He drilled her about who she was spending time with or why a strange guy would smile at her.

He capitalized on the strained relationship with her mom, and the growing distance between her and other friends and family. He kept her isolated and controlled how she spent her time. He became physically aggressive, and eventually thought nothing of raising his hand as a threat. She stopped accepting calls and responding to text and Facebook messages. It took a while to realize he had been deleting them and erasing her call history.

Shantay was a bright and accomplished young woman. Maybe she was reluctant to admit that her first romantic relationship had been a catastrophe. Rationally, she understood right from wrong. But the abusive behavior of her early childhood triggered a deep-seated sense of hopelessness and desolation. Kevin's verbal and physical assaults chipped away at the love and acceptance Michaela had instilled. Isolated from loved ones and positive affirmation, she was unable to resist the intrusive onslaught of lies beaten into her by her first adoptive mother. In the wake of frequent violent outbursts, accusing statements reverberated from deep within her: You are disgusting. No one wants you. You are disposable. You get exactly what you deserve. You are unlovable. She felt trapped, paralyzed by fear, and returned to the familiar and instinctive responses that kept her alive when she was young. Make yourself small, maybe you can appease the monster and avoid the wrath.

A few times Shantay found the strength to break it off. But Kevin knew how to lure her back. Flowers, declarations of love, begging for her forgiveness, and promising to never hit her again. When that was ineffective, he reminded her how it was her actions that provoked him, twisting the truth, and convincing her she was to blame.

By the time Michaela told me about the abuse, she was not sure how long it had been going on. Shantay had finally confided in her during a video chat. She recounted their first honest conversation in years.

"Rick, you should have seen her. It was obvious she had been crying hysterically. Her eyes were swollen, and she kept blowing her nose. I asked her what was wrong; what had happened. With her voice faltering, she finally let me in.

"Kevin had just stormed out of their apartment after forcing himself on her. She told me he does that every day. It did not matter whether she was studying or late for class or when he got home late after drinking. When he wanted to have sex, and she did not feel well or was tired, he would not stop. It was hard to hear her admitting these things and it was just as difficult for her to share them. She was afraid I would be disappointed but needed to know I still loved her.

42

"Rick, I tried to stay calm, and was careful how I responded. She told me their intimacy had been fun in the beginning. Being with him made her feel special. Then she began to sob and said she could not remember feeling happy. She had been so sure of herself and now she feels like her dreams of becoming a counselor were slipping through her fingers.

"Kevin suddenly came back into the apartment, and she hung up without a word. It was more than a week before I heard from her again. When I answered the video chat Kevin was sitting beside her. She had taken a pregnancy test and they were sharing the news that she was having a baby. Then, with head hung and him looking at her and not me, she apologized for calling before and saying all kinds of crazy things. Now she knew she was crying and exhausted and acting paranoid because she was pregnant.

"I feigned a smile, but I was crushed."

CHAPTER 8

The morning after the memorial I felt emotionally hungover. Without saying a word, Becky had pushed our plans to the afternoon giving me time to recoup. I built a fire, refilled my iced tea, and leaned back in the recliner.

I knew if I did not distract myself, I would certainly spin out in a vortex of rumination. But resistance was in vain. Fatigue had taken a position squarely on my heart, and motivation surrendered without a fight. I was desperate for this to not be the end of her story. If I were still in law enforcement, I don't know how I would have returned to the battle.

I had recommended that Shantay consider telling her story and authoring a book. She lit up when we discussed the multifaceted positive outcomes that would occur. I explained how inspiring it would be to other survivors, and the detectives and social workers fighting to rescue other children. I told her every person who read her story would be moved by her resilience and bravery. Even people in the community who were reluctant to report suspected abuse would find the courage to speak up. Her story had the power to save other children.

She dreamed of such a day, but wanted to have her bachelor's degree in hand before she considered it. Her confidence did not include exposing such personal information, fearing others would reject her. She had been taught that purpose beyond understanding could come from her pain, but she never understood what that meant. Her faith also taught her that true victory comes when we take our stories out of the darkness and share them fearlessly in the light.

Even though her name had been legally changed a third time, she was still fearful of the Hunters. The prospect of seeing them or provoking them petrified her. She agreed that one day she would tell the entire world her story.

I tried to explain that being taught about abuse is quite different than hearing about it from an adult survivor. She also had experienced the beautiful rescue into a new family. It might encourage more families to become foster parents or to adopt foster children. She saw glimpses of abundant fruit where only seeds of devastation had once been sown. She wanted to shout to the world that victimization did not define her.

Now her story will never be told as only she could have. Thousands of people that should have known this beautiful and valiant woman, will never hear her message of hope.

Becky came into the den with her coat buttoned, scarf wrapped around her neck and gloves in hand. I roused myself from a stupor of languishing. "Hey Beck, where are you headed?" I asked.

"To the post office to mail a few packages. I won't be long. Sweetheart, I love you. I cannot imagine what you are going through. I know you are hurting, and I am not sure what to say." She bent down to kiss me and lingered for a moment. "Have you spoken to Mike this week? You should give him a call."

My brother lives out of state, so I was able to share more behind the scenes challenges I was facing. He and Jami were confidants that helped carry the burdens I shielded from my family. His perspective included a lifetime of knowledge and a shared family heritage. We speak weekly, and we discuss everything. He joined the U.S. Marines out of high school and started college while in the Marines. His grades were such that he accepted the challenge to enter medical school. For good measure he double majored, adding literature to his repertoire in the process. He chose a path of serving his community as a physician, and ultimately retired from the Navy as a Radiologist.

"How's my favorite big brother?" Mike asked enthusiastically when he answered the phone. "You know I am your only brother," I reminded him with a chuckle. "Yeah, but you are still my favorite. I cannot let you forget that. How was your week? Are you looking forward to the Holiday?" he asked.

"The weekend had been booked with Santa photo shoots. I had to reschedule; I just do not have it in me to smile and say 'Ho, Ho, Ho' like all is right in the world."

The Christmases my brother and I experienced were magical. Even as we became adults the joy of Christmas persisted. After retiring from law enforcement, I grew my beard out. It was snow white. Then I decided to dress in upscale Santa Claus attire and offer to pose for professional photo sessions with families. The popularity of an authentic looking Santa launched a fun idea into a high demand "side-gig" with the added bonus of relishing in the childlike wonder of Christmas. Eventually bookings filled every weekend from mid-October to early December. My brother was not surprised when I shared how successful it had become. He said it made perfect sense that I would become Santa Claus, given our childhood Christmases. He then jokingly began referring to himself as "Fred Claus".

"Mike, do you remember me telling you about that young woman who was murdered a couple of weeks ago, the case I worked over a decade ago? Her memorial service was last night. There was a great turn out, and I was glad for the family. But you know how I hate funerals. I talked with her mom for a long while. I saw most of the family. I had not seen them since her graduation. And you know how different I look from my years wearing the badge. The whole Santa Claus white hair caused some to do a double take.

"Mike, I met her little girl, Anna. She is only three years old. The child was with Michaela when she found Shantay's body. I have been stressed out for weeks and last night was the culmination. Everyone is grieving without closure."

My brother responded as a great brother would. He listened, commiserated, and offered support. There was no fixing this. I was hurting, and he knew no logic or reasoning would lessen the loss or ease the pain. I was grateful to know our families would be together in a few weeks.

When the call ended, I added some wood to the fire and reclined in the chair. I felt calmer. I closed my eyes refreshed by everything my brother's voice evokes. This time I drifted back to the wholesomeness of our "Mayberry" childhood. The place I first experienced a sense of perfect well-being.

~

My family grew up country poor. Every need was met but there were few extras. We never considered ourselves poor because life was not measured by possessions. The first thirteen years of my life our family lived in an older single wide mobile home. My dad's parents were our neighbors on one side, and his brother and family were the neighbors on the other. Our collective was tucked away, off the beaten path, down a long dirt road and beside a stream. We lived in rural Callaghan, an unincorporated community in Allegheny County Virginia. We had the smallest population of six neighboring communities within a 5-mile radius. In 2020 the population had dwindled to 247.

In the early 1970s a steady stream of modern technology and conveniences were becoming part of the American lifestyle. Each new gadget was presented as a complementary addendum to the evolving American dream. The fads sweeping across the nation, and transforming the culture, rarely reached our rural community. Radio and TV commercials steadily primed listeners to believe they were missing something others were enjoying. A fast-changing world was evolving beyond our modest lifestyle. When modern appliances trickled into the local mercantile it was long after much of the hullabaloo died down. We were content with what we had.

Except for a small crossroads in town, the county was rural. Property lines spread everywhere with dozens or hundreds of acres between. Most families had lived in the area for generations.

Grandpa was the only one that enjoyed frequent company. Visitors were forced to maneuver carefully down a long dirt lane from the byway to our trailers. Drought conditions turned the rocky surface into a powder-fine dust bowl. Heavy rain collected in the deep ruts forming mud pits that could sink tires to their rims. Once a year dad would plow around the potholes and try to even out the worst spots. The remoteness prevented mom from enjoying nearby friends while we were in school. Occasionally she picked up part-time work, mostly to help with annual clothes shopping or if a merchant needed an extra hand. She never left the house before the bus picked us up and was always home after school.

Throughout my early childhood, dad worked brutal hours and barely scratched out a living. He landed a job at the Hercules plant, one of the primary employers in town. The schedule mandated long shift work at night. Mom always had a meal prepared for his return. He would scarf down food, glance at the paper, and head to bed. We were expected to be quiet or go outdoors. It was not what he wanted for his family, but it was the price he paid to provide.

When we were older dad began laying brick and stone. His skills as a stone mason excelled. As his reputation for excellence spread, opportunities for work expanded beyond the community. He began to travel. Many weeks he left before dawn on Monday and did not return until after dinner on Friday.

My folks managed what they had without complaining, at least not in front of us. We learned how to rely on one another. Gratitude for the provisions we had turned scarcity into plenty. Mom had a knack for multiplying and stretching resources.

Our day centered around a hearty evening meal. Mom fixed all sorts of wild game: squirrel, wild turkey, coon, rabbit, and venison. We were country folks, and everyone ate what they hunted so I thought nothing of it. In fact, one of my favorite meals was rabbit gravy and biscuits. That was a rare treat though because I never got the hang of leading rabbits.

Every other Thursday when dad got paid, mom took Mike and I with her to the grocery store. Once dad was asleep, Mom would gather us up and head into town. After she cashed his check, we ventured to the grocery store. My eyes would discreetly scan the rows of boxed cereal when she reached for the bulk containers of oatmeal and cream of wheat. We never asked for any, but I am sure she noticed. Mom made sacrifices too, but we were not old enough to understand that at the time. Mom could make anything special. Mike has described our mother as "someone who could make a shoe box feel like home and can make gravy from dishwater." And it is true.

Our bi-weekly outing was an occasion to celebrate. As far back as I remember we enjoyed a special tradition; the day mom bought groceries we feasted on burgers for the evening meal. Juicy, delicious beef burgers cooked in a frying pan or on the grill every other Thursday, a cadence as dependable as sunrise. Those simple but loving rhythms permeated our childhood. Mike and I recall that tradition every time we fire up the grill. Those delicious patties represented assurance and comfort. The unspoken symbolism that accompanied burger night was, life is good, and we would be okay for two more weeks. To this day, there is nothing like a perfectly grilled hamburger!

Sundays and Wednesday evenings you would find us gathered with a small congregation at the local Baptist Church. When the church hosted bible school during summer, mom ensured we attended. After church on Sunday, we drove forty miles to our other grandparents' farm in Smoot, West Virginia. Mom was one of seventeen children, most of whom brought their broods to partake of their family supper tradition. Grandmom would prepare a huge meal. Copious dishes of fresh fixings from her bountiful garden, and homemade bread, rolls or biscuits. We feasted and amused ourselves with dozens of cousins. Everyone stayed all afternoon. When night fell, the vast sky was filled with stars, and we chased fireflies. In summer we lingered even longer and played until our hearts were content. Adults drank lemonade and fanned themselves staving off the oppressive heat discussing who knows what.

Grandmom was the matriarch, and as constant as the northern star. She guided her family through thick and thin. She held everyone together with an endearing wit and exuberant sense of humor. Her laughter was contagious, and no matter how 'off' your mood was, she could make you laugh. The grandkids loved being around her. During summer break, she divided time with the older grandkids, affording each one focused time and attention. I would spend a week, sometimes two, every summer. Mornings came early on the farm, and my days were filled with milking cows, hauling hay, mucking out stables, and carrying water and wood into the house. Grandmom always served homemade cottage cheese and pickled beets especially for me. I loved being there. They never invested in indoor plumbing, so at the farm we used an outhouse. What a hoot that could be on Sunday afternoons!

Grandad and grandpa were both coal miners in their younger years. That was a primary source of employment in the post-depression era. I am not sure what was worse; the horrible conditions they worked in or shutting the mine down which forced families out of company housing and into dire straits. Before I was born, my grandad was injured in a mining accident. The company awarded him $5,000 for his severed finger, which they used to buy the farm. Black lung robbed much of his vigor, and he died much younger than he should have.

Grandad was more like a stranger, and unapproachable to the grandkids. We all avoided him. You could set your watch to his bedtime. Summer or winter, he went to bed at 8 o'clock every night. He would walk away from our huge family gathering without a word. On long summer days when daylight stretches gently into night, we would play for as long as we could. Swarming in circles around our parents, and the nearby fields, taking turns on the big tire swing and playing tag or hide and go seek. Whoever was "it" would count loud enough for everyone scattering in opposite directions to hear. The giggles of younger kids could be heard. The teasing laughter of the older ones when they were caught filled the atmosphere. Grandad would get annoyed and firmly smack his bedroom window. "That is enough! Y'all hush so I can sleep."

In the stifling summer heat, we would crank the handles of every window in the trailer wide open. Then we would leave our bedroom doors open hoping to catch a cross breeze. Lying still waiting for the air to cool, we were lulled by nature's orchestra. Bullfrogs, crickets, cicada, katydids, and hoot owls all played their parts. The nocturnal wildlife that receded by day appeared from obscurity by night. The pulsating mantra of insects was interrupted by sporadic wails, howling, and shrieks of coyotes; and foxes prowling about. Raccoons and possums flaunted their presence rummaging for morsels nearby.

Living beside a stream was excellent for fishing and cooling off in July and August. I cast a fishing line into those waters a million times over the years. The proximity to the creek bed meant the ground around our property was chocked-full of rocks. After grandpa's first heart attack, he was weaker and less surefooted. Dad devised a plan to remove tripping hazards and volunteered me for the task. What started as a project to clear a path spread to an ever-widening perimeter. Leveling the ground required digging up countless protruding rocks. Many of the stones were deeply embedded. Removing them seemed impossible and impractical. The hours I spent carving away the crusty earth and digging deep enough to remove them is incalculable. Was dad trying to teach me an obscure lesson through this dreaded task or simply passing on grunt work? I have no idea. This fruitless endeavor aggravated me. At the beginning I complained and dragged my feet every time.

As retrospect often reveals, this detested manual labor helped remove a few inner obstacles within me. It also shored up characteristics that would prove durable. As the rocks I strategically placed along the eroding creek banks increased, so did my work ethic and ability to fit pieces together. Excuses and haphazard efforts gradually gave way to determination. Perseverance forged patience. Stubborn obstacles provoked resourcefulness. Basic problem solving expanded my ability to think beyond the obvious. Countless hours that produced minimal results began to offer a vague sense of accomplishment.

Grandpa and I shared many quiet times with no one else around. Watching deer graze freely in the fields on either side of the dirt road. Young bucks displayed their strength and agility bounding gracefully across the field. Grandpa and I would settle into a stand on the edge of the woodlands. For hours we sat in silence watching their rituals. Scraping and making territory and engaging in dangerous sparring they would compete for domination and to impress the doe. In spring we watched does with their new fawn. There was nothing like seeing the cycle of life for these beautiful creatures.

Winters in the mountains could leave us happily stranded for days. When snow and ice-covered roads became impassable, schools would close, and we would go deer hunting or sled down the hill in front of our trailer for hours.

CHAPTER 9

Grandpa's willingness to fill the gap created by dad working nights and sleeping days was pivotal. I never knew if he decided to do so naturally or if he and mom discussed it. What I do know is that during that time I learned the truest measures of wealth were not based on income or limited by a lack of possessions.

Grandpa never pretended money was not important. He was acquainted with the challenges of sustaining a family on meager means. He lived through the depression and felt the pangs of hunger and running low on firewood in the winter. He survived squalid conditions and bore the burden of watching his family suffer. During prohibition he had a moonshine still hidden in a remote area in the Allegheny mountains. He was renowned for his ability to produce what many considered the best "white lightening" and "corn squeezins" ever made. Not a soul he knew had seen him drink a drop. "Shine's for supporting the family, not for making me act a fool." He would tell me stories about those days with a grin on his face reserved for those conversations. He said even the feds, he called them "stabs," knew of his reputation for distributing quality drink.

One day they finally caught up with him. He said he took off running like a rabbit being chased by a fox. They shot in his direction a few times, but their aim was no match for his startled response and the surge of adrenaline it induced. One shot hit his hand. He told me it knocked him to the ground, but he jumped back up and kept running. Since they never caught him, they could not prove the still was his, and he was never charged. When they busted up his still, that was the end of that. Many of his regular visitors were the older men who had bought jars of moonshine back in the day.

He had worked the coal mines for decades, like most men in those parts. Black lung got the best of him, and he had to quit working in the mid 60's. I had only known him at home each day. Instead of talking about what we did not have, he challenged the idea that money defined a man or proved his character. He confronted the societal definitions of poverty and wealth and the fallacy that our purpose in life was linked to income. He exemplified a life of gratitude. He adjusted the lens through which we viewed ambitions and priorities. He was beloved in the community and friends were always stopping by. Grandpa's sage wisdom governed my childhood. His legacy, a wealth no money could buy.

I was older than my brother and many adventures were just grandpa and me. We shared a passion for being outdoors; hunting, fishing, whatever. Inclement weather never deterred us from whatever adventure we planned. I learned to use rifles and shotguns at an early age, and we went rabbit and coon hunting year-round just to hear the dog's trail. On summer nights, he would take me out long after dark. "Come on, boy; let's find us some coons." In a shroud of darkness, we used instinct and moonlight to guide us. He would wear his carbide light from old-time mining days, with a single flame on the top of his hat as the only source of light. We would wander down paths we had memorized to carefully curated places in the woods.

On a clear night when the moon was waning, the black skies were illuminated like a celestial garden. The constellations declared something I had no language for. The sky was a vast sea of ink speckled with an infinite number of stars twinkling with approval. I wondered if God had scattered the galaxies with these shimmering lights and then intricately placed each planet like an ornament on a tree. Or were the stars tossed like glitter after setting each planet in its place. Whatever held these answers to this unknown mystery, it was the stunning backdrop to my midnight adventures.

Perhaps our similar temperaments contributed to the natural ease between me and my grandpa. But our connection was deeper. Even in the awkwardness of pre-adolescence, I was comfortable being myself. He didn't just love me, he liked me. I could ask him any question. He never criticized or made me feel silly or say I was too young to ask such things. His calming presence never wavered. He became the plumbline to which I tethered myself. Grandpa never forced his opinion, but it mattered more than anyone else's. My curious mind was hungry for the wisdom he offered.

He believed in me and my brother, and it empowered us to believe anything was possible. I know my dad did too, but his generation expressed their love by supporting the family. When I reflect on my childhood, I can picture the cluster of mobile homes and glasses of watery milk. But I also see a loving family that made a simple life extraordinary. And I see the gift of a grandpa who weighed his words carefully, who understood his grandsons would go further than they could ever have imagined. He saw boundless potential in two scruffy headed kids in overalls with dirty feet. He mentored and shaped me like the potter's hands, firmly but gently guiding the impressionable clay.

Grandpa was a man of his word, as loyal as a summer day is long. The roots of security and belonging grew deep within. Being in his company instilled as much in me as the wealth of wisdom he shared in conversation. He never tried to impress me; he never needed to. The finest characteristics of this giant of a man, are the same I desired to emulate. Decades of living had been his classroom. His body had been strong once, and formidable from decades of long days of heavy labor in risky environments and conditions that compromised his health. He had lived through summers of drought and widespread crop failures. He had watched gardens flourish into a bounty of provision for his family. He had lived through devastating floods when torrential rains caused every tributary to swell beyond its natural boundaries sweeping homes downstream. He lived through the depression era, wars, and great personal tragedy. He endured physical decline and failing health. Yet he never ceased being grateful for the beauty of life.

Even now, when the stress and pressure press in, I return to the cadence and stride of his footprint. It always brings peace and clarity.

~

Dad's mom was the opposite of his father. In every way he was loving and patient, she was cantankerous and impetuous. Her responses were antagonistic, and we learned to muzzle our opinions around her. When she was on a rampage, no one was spared. We often heard her provoke and berate grandpa, controlling and directing his every move. As much as I enjoyed his company, I avoided hers. He never spoke a harsh word against her even though she made everyone's life harder. Tempted as we were at times to ask questions or comment, the unmerited respect he extended to her was a powerful lesson.

Grandpa never went to church. He must have found his God while fishing or sitting in the woods surrounded by nature. The earth, nature and simple pleasures grounded him.

Grandma belonged to a church vastly different than the one my family attended. I do not recall why, but I visited her church one time when I was 4 or 5. I remember it like yesterday, and I never went again. She attended one of those wild churches where the preacher yells the whole time. I was not sure if he was screaming at the devil or trying to scare the devil out of people. Whichever it was, it was not working because he never stopped. He was pacing, sweating, flailing his hands and arms like a crazy man. He would thump his bible on the pulpit so hard it made me jump. People were whooping, hollering, and running around like someone was chasing them. A bunch of adults were wailing and talking gibberish. I was frightened and traumatized. I dropped to the ground and squeezed under the pew to hide. I curled up on my knees, my face to the floor, eyes closed and covered my ears. It only muffled the hysteria that seemed to go on forever. That terrifying encounter with religion took me to the edge of reluctance, and another early childhood experience pushed me over.

I attended Callaghan Elementary, in Covington from 1st grade through 7th grade. At the time there was no kindergarten and high school started in the 8th grade. In the 1970's schools still offered daily prayer, and the teachers were permitted to utilize corporal punishment. Each class entered the cafeteria, students picked up their trays and filed to their assigned tables. No one ate until the entire class was seated. Someone would be assigned to ring a bell placed on the edge of every table and lead prayer. When the bell was rung the whole cafeteria would go quiet. The student assigned that day would lead the prayer. "God is great, God is good" and the class would join in. The day I was leader for the week brought the most embarrassing moment of elementary school. When the bell rang, the words that proceeded from my lips were "Our Father which art in Heaven, hallowed be thy name." By the time I realized I was saying the Lord's prayer I quickly switched to the "correct" prayer. Not a soul mentioned it, ever. But it was the first time I felt embarrassed, and the memory is visceral. I never offered to pray openly again.

~

Not long before grandpa died, grandma spoiled a family gathering with one of her tirades. Later that day, grandpa sat me and my brother down. He sat across from us, lowered his face to eye level and moved in close. His face was tan and leathery from decades in the sun. Deep grooves etched his face like a map. Whiskers poked out from his chin and upper lip where he had not shaved in days. His hair remained dark even at his age. The years had curved his shoulders downward and slowed his pace. But his stature transcended age, his voice carried authority and his eyes twinkled like Santa Claus. He delighted in us, and we knew it.

57

"Boys, I am not making excuses for your grandma. I am sorry she ruined the picnic. Your grandma is a hard pill to swallow. I know boys, I do. I wish to heaven it were different. I wish you knew the girl I married. She had a smile as big as the moon and as bright as the sun. She was the prettiest thing I had ever seen. I loved her back then and I love her still. Even though it does not always seem that way, your grandma loves y'all to. And, as disagreeable as she can be with your momma, she loves her too.

"When I married your grandma, we were just kids. We did not know anything about life, too young to understand that tough times were bound to come. But that day I promised to love her for better or for worse and I have been doing that every day since. Even when it is not easy. Boys, your grandma and me, we had good years, there are lots of good memories tucked in my heart. I think about those and that promise I made to that young girl. That is what keeps me going."

I never forgot his words, but I wondered what caused her to become so embittered. If grandpa knew, he took it to his grave. As an adult I understood that people bring their childhood into marriage. Disappointment and hardship can sour someone's disposition and broken trust cannot always be mended. Tragedy can create irreconcilable differences between people who once deeply loved each other. Divorce was rare in his generation and not something he ever considered.

My brother and I could have been disillusioned and apprehensive about marriage. Something about grandpa's words that day and watching him return a soft word for his wife's sharp tongue, and salty comments mystified me. In simple man's terms, he learned to pay her no mind. In truth, he refused to take her belligerent eruptions personally.

Mind you, when his tolerance of her controlling reached a limit, he knew how to rein her back in. He would call her by her full name.

Sometimes he had to say it twice with a slightly elevated volume. It was like interrupting a tornado. When her eyes met his beneath a lifted eyebrow, his request was articulated without words. She would mumble under her breath, brush her hands across her apron in protest, and walk away. His bride had aged into an insufferable dictator, who made life hard for everyone. He chose to rise above the fray.

Mom and grandma would go toe-to-toe sometimes. With us and in our home, she chose to battle with serenity and to fill our home and her responses with love and kindness. Mom and grandpa were more invested in keeping the peace that perpetuated our sense of well-being.

CHAPTER 10

Shortly after grandpa passed, we packed our possessions and moved to Fairdale, West Virginia. Mom's relationship with my grandma further deteriorated after grandpa was no longer a buffer or mediator. His absence made living next door to her intolerable. I do not know if we would have moved otherwise, but it served as the catalyst and set us on a new path. As much as my grandma offended and hurt my mom, a few years after we moved, she had a stroke. Not a soul in her family would lend a hand. She had burned a lot of bridges. To mom's monumental credit, she agreed to bring grandma into our home where she could take care of her. The stroke robbed Grandma of her memory, her feistiness and ability to communicate well.

The population of Fairdale West Virginia was not much larger than Callaghan, but it was brand new, and we lived closer to everything.

Mike is 2 ½ years younger than me but we were thick as thieves. The bond forged in youth lasted beyond the separate paths we chose after high school. We are still close and talk every week. Together we learned the value of hard work, loyalty, and integrity. Our humble beginning instilled core values and tenets that have carried us through adulthood.

Thrust into a new community, and me on the cusp of high school, our response to this transition could have gone either way. We embraced every drop of potential it offered. Living closer to town and school we were no longer constrained to being home afternoons and weekends. We integrated quickly and filled our time exploring extracurricular and social activities. My brother and I felt like we had rubbed the genie out of the bottle and many wishes were granted. For the first time relationships extended beyond immediate family and reached beyond classroom hours. One junior and senior high school combined with mutual activities, created an ideal crossover of friends.

We harnessed the work ethic ingrained in us as young men and channeled it into our athletic pursuits. My brother excelled in baseball and wrestling. His fierce commitment propelled him, and he advanced quickly. When he graduated, he was offered a choice of scholarships. Ironically, he turned them all down to follow a deeper passion, joining the United States Marine Corp. Semper Fidelis "Always Faithful;" that is my brother to a T.

The dedication, patience and persistence modeled by our grandpa served us well as we explored hobbies and talents. I played football in the fall and baseball in the spring. I also picked up the saxophone and discovered an unexplored knack for music. In between sports I auditioned for the school band. Over the years I mastered the baritone saxophone and progressed through all American, all regional and state level competitions. My ancillary hobby became one of my highest achievements. Many favorite memories revolve around those events. The pinnacle of my band experience occurred the summer after graduation. I was selected to take part in the United States Collegiate Wind Band and the ensemble toured seven countries throughout Europe.

The most significant gift that resulted from our move was meeting Becky. I was a junior and she was a first-year student at another high school. Our meeting was the storyline scripted for countless romantic movies. Two young people meet by chance, the attraction that feels like magic, they become high school sweethearts and find love and friendship that lasts a lifetime. Honestly, from the day we started hanging out we never looked back. It was a defining moment in our lives.

We planned to pick up my brother's girlfriend, then pick up the girl I was dating before I met Becky. We would all go to the theater for a double date. Our plans were thwarted when my girlfriend got in trouble and her dad refused to allow her to leave. My brother was not about to have his plans spoiled, so we headed to his girlfriend's house anyway. Unexpectedly without a date, his girlfriend asked if her cousin could ride along. The fourteen-year-old cousin visiting from another school district was my sweet Becky. I will never forget that night. We saw the movie "Empire of the Ants" with Joan Collins. From that first evening, we began talking by phone and spending as much time together as possible. Strange how things work out, how there is always a bigger plan and at any moment the unexpected becomes a new beginning.

My parents loved Becky and she integrated into our family famously. Her family was not as close, and she welcomed the affection and sense of belonging she found with my family.

~

When I returned from my whirlwind European adventure with the Wind Ensemble, I set my sights on an electronics program in Charleston. The technical school offered students certification in various high demand, blue-collar trades. Successful completion would pave the way to an above average salary and a promising future. Charleston was twenty-five times the size of my hometown. The opportunities seemed limitless but a bit overwhelming. I wasn't taken in by all the advantages of the city that were enticing many young adults to flee from rural areas of West Virginia. My generation was being baptized into the "outside world." Even those who were not interested in big city life had their sights set on more than rural living, factory work and farming.

I aced the electronics courses but even with the promise of reliable work, and a lucrative income the prospect of this trade as a career was not personally satisfying. After exploring options, I decided to join the fire department in Beckley, West Virginia. At the age of nineteen, I became the youngest paid firefighter in the department. Becky and I began building a life together separately but together as independent adults.

For six years I served as a firefighter. As I wrestled with the aspects of the job I did not enjoy, my professional discontent was countered by a blissful personal life. It had not been my choice to move to West Virginia and it was not where I wanted to be.

When I asked Becky to become my wife, I had been pondering our future in new and more mature ways. We knew early on that we would get married, but nothing about our relationship was forced or pressured by a timeline. My career goals were unsettled, and my desires still evolving. Wanting to become her husband never wavered. We both wanted to have children young, and our perceptions and expectations of marriage meshed well.

We enjoyed several years as a carefree couple. When I was ready to propose, I knew planning an elaborate event that culminated in a public spectacle was out of the question. An extravagant proposal would not have suited her personality, nor did it embody the natural course of our relationship. The ring I purchased was not ornate, but she was radiant when she saw it. I had visited several jewelers before making my final selection. I set aside part of every paycheck and made payments for months in advance. Then I waited until Christmas.

Christmas morning the landscape was blanketed in pure tranquility. Snow had fallen lightly overnight, and snow was expected to continue all day. I headed to Becky's place in my 4-wheel drive jeep. We had squeezed the Christmas tree into her small apartment, having to push it against the only large window to make it fit. Thick snowflakes continued falling in a gentle hush. The scene being scripted by mother nature created a Currier and Ives backdrop for the day. Multi-colored lights on the tree blinked in a slow and steady tempo that matched the pace of the morning. Christmas music played on the FM station, uninterrupted by commercials.

I cooked breakfast while Becky heated the tea kettle and set the table for two. She laughed when I placed a heaping platter of French toast in the center of the table. I had lightly dusted it with confectioners' sugar and drizzled the top with warm maple syrup. "How are we supposed to eat all that?" she asked lightheartedly. "Thank you for making breakfast honey. This looks delicious," she said after kissing my cheek.

With our hearts and bellies full, we moved to the couch and turned our attention to the gifts beneath the tree. The scent of Fraser fir mingled with the lingering aroma of breakfast. Gifts were placed sparsely around the tree skirt. "Which one should I open first?" she asked. "You decide," I responded, not wanting to alert her or prompt suspicion. We took turns selecting packages and opening them one at a time. I felt a bit euphoric, which may have been accentuated by syrup and caffeine. I could not wait to see her response, but I wanted the moment to unfold naturally. She opened each gift slowly and methodically trying not to tear the paper, relishing the day.

She opened a set of three mixed tapes I made for her, a compilation of our current favorites and popular hits the year we began dating. I opened a box with new gloves. She had seen me admiring them when we were shopping and went back later. Back and forth we opened presents until she finally selected the package I had discretely over-boxed to conceal its contents. She pulled each thin strand of ribbon. She lifted the edges of wrapping paper from all four sides and set it aside. She used my pocketknife to cut through the tape securing the top. She lifted the flaps and peered inside to find wads of crinkled newspaper. She pulled several out and then dug around until her fingers touched the smaller box. She drew it from its hiding place, looked at me and smiled with pure delight. The moment was as simple and perfect, the kind of moments we built our lives upon.

Eight months later I married the love of my life. Our closest friends and family gathered at the small country church Becky attended as a child. My lovely bride wore a full-length white lace dress, with sheer sleeves and neckline. I sported a white suit with tails. Her veil was gathered and attached to a lace hat, cascading gracefully down her back to hip length. Her bouquet was a simple bundle of white daisies and baby's breath tied with strands of white ribbon that dangled below. I was twenty-one years old, and she was eighteen.

My brother was my best man. My cousin played background music on the piano as guests were filling the pews. When the ebony and ivory keys began to ring out the wedding march, guests rose to the prompting. Turning toward the double doors in the back of the chapel we waited for Becky to appear. The doors swung open, and my gorgeous bride was standing in the doorway beside her uncle. Becky's father passed away from cancer when she was seven years old. Her mother never remarried, and her uncle was the closest to a father figure. Taking his arm, she began walking toward me. I never looked away, memorizing her face, and mirroring her smile.

Prior to exchanging vows, we stood side by side holding hands at the altar. We selected "There is Love," by Peter, Paul, and Mary as the only song to be played during the ceremony. My cousin softly strummed his acoustic guitar and sung the popular wedding song. I could not imagine being happier. When the chapel went quiet, we turned to face one another, and the pastor led us in our pledge of mutual love and commitment.

In ideal country style, our families combined resources and prepared a hearty potluck for the reception meal. Everyone feasted and enjoyed the afternoon free from the stress of fanfare and formality. Her wedding dress was a gift from her mother. I bought the cake, and Becky paid for the flowers and invitations. All told, the celebration cost less than $500.

Our honeymoon was a camping adventure at Moomaw Lake. My brother drove to the camp site and set everything up in advance. The drive was an hour and a half, and we decided to leave the next day to arrive during daylight. On the way we stopped to fill up at the last gas station before the lake, still 45 minutes out. That's when I first noticed the smell of gasoline, I did not think twice. I drove an older jeep and that was not particularly unusual. After several trips back and forth from the jeep to the camp site throughout the day, I was aware that the smell had not subsided. A quick glance revealed an area of moisture on the ground beneath the gas tank. Poking my head underneath for a closer glance and a potent whiff confirmed a leak. Gas droplets were slipping through a pin-size hole.

How did that happen and how did I miss it? I turned the key to check the gauge, the leak was not significant but measurable. We decided not to take a chance and only spent one night before heading back to our life as Mr. & Mrs.

We recently celebrated our 40th anniversary and still enjoy being together as much as we did in our youth.

CHAPTER 11

When Becky and I were ready to expand our family, we had no idea it would take three years for her to conceive. We supported one another, tried to remain optimistic, and agreed to trust the timing. The delay intensified our desire, longing to welcome a baby into the rhythm of our lives. Our anticipation increased and we grew stronger as a couple. When her doctor finally confirmed the pregnancy test was positive, we were elated. We called our out-of-town family and shared the news with friends and co-workers. We embraced our next adventure into unfamiliar territory.

I imagined sharing the news with my grandpa. His eyes filled with gentle knowing and his crooked smile beaming with expectancy. I was honored to be part of his legacy and understood that it came with responsibility. I had experienced life on the receiving end of his generosity. It was my turn to embody a sacrificial lifestyle and impart those moral attributes to the next generation.

We agreed that Beckley, West Virginia was not where we wanted to begin our family. The time to make that change was now. I knew she trusted me; we were in this together. For both our sakes, I needed to resolve the restlessness I was feeling. My passion for public safety had remained but expanded to careers beyond the fire department. While batting options, an advertisement appeared in the local paper for young men interested in becoming police officers. The department was 4 hours east in south central Virginia and the academy would begin in October. No one on my crew was familiar with the area, but I decided to take my chances and applied.

The department required potential candidates to pass a written exam and physical test prior to applying. My brother and our families were camping. On Sunday morning we got up and I decided to go take the test. We packed our camping gear as quickly as possible and headed home to drop off the families. By the time we had arrived home and unpacked it was about 6PM. We grabbed dinner and headed out. Mike and I took turns driving through the night arriving at 3AM in the parking lot of the high school where testing would take place. We slept in the back of the truck until daybreak. Testing started at 7AM. I completed the written exam and physical test with little sleep. Fueled by anticipation and adrenaline, I gutted through both, and scored well enough to be accepted for the academy and into the career for which I felt destined.

Becky knew I was drawn to law enforcement, but we never discussed relocating so far. Moving would be a tremendous sacrifice for her. It was a stressful time to introduce the possibility of such a drastic transition. I was asking her to leave friends, family, and her job a few months before childbirth. We would shift from preparing the nursery to packing, finding a home in an unfamiliar community, and setting up household before her due date.

Her mother worked full time and would be unable to help with a newborn. We would be too far from friends who could prepare meals or lend a hand as she navigated the early days of motherhood. It was a big ask. If the prospect had not been so appealing, I would never have considered suggesting we uproot our lives.

It took several weeks for the recruiter to respond to my inquiry. A letter inviting me to join the academy finally appeared in the mailbox. During that time there were many conversations. Becky has always championed my desire to enjoy my career. She was fully supportive and did not resist or bemoan how it would affect her as a first-time mother. Accepting that she would be isolated from everyone except me did not deter her. Facing challenges together was an unrivaled priority. If we had understood how demanding the academy would be, we might have waited. It was an extremely difficult season for her. She spent long hours at home alone. When I was physically present, I was often distracted while studying. It was a lonely chapter in her life, and I have some regrets for causing that. If you asked her, she has none. She grew as a woman, a wife, and a mother. Having only one another to rely upon strengthened our bond. She would say the move was the best thing that could have happened to our marriage, and it was all worth it in the end.

~

The individuals drawn to law enforcement are a distinctive breed. The motto "to serve and protect" attracts the lion's share of motivated, disciplinary, type-A personalities. The kind of self-driven, goal-oriented, focused mavericks whose accomplishments tend to accentuate individuality verses teamwork.

I have seen my share of hot heads that groused and blamed leadership instead of becoming part of the solution. I have watched decent officers unable to bridle their egos. Younger officers confronted by disciplinary action either moved on or accepted responsibility and grew up. But contrary to the narrative perpetuated by the media vilifying all law enforcement officers based on the horrendous actions of a small number of bad cops, the vast majority of those who have answered the call are the finest consortium of brave, resolute, and sacrificial humans I have known.

Unbeknownst to me, the dynamics of my boyhood pre-disposed me to seek fulfillment in a culture of excellence, integrity, and solidarity of purpose. The attributes that served me well in firefighting and later in law enforcement were traceable to my grandpa's influence. A childlike admiration birthed a determination to emulate the man I held in highest esteem. My pre-teen years were the tale of a country boy learning what it means to be a man. Grandpa's rugged but humble confidence continued to influence me years after he passed. I returned to the riverbank and listened for his voice when I became a husband, changed careers, relocated my family, and became a father. I miss him enormously and know our lives would be even richer if he were still here.

I learned to deescalate situations by keeping a clear head. I excelled at observing behaviors and absorbing details without reacting. I earned the respect of co-workers and my career progressed. In time, opportunities that I could not have orchestrated were presented. We never imagined where the winds of change would carry us. As my career evolved, my skills expanded through progressively increased responsibility. Duties required me to continually shift the practical application of my family as priority.

The first years as a police officer, I worked midnight shift on the Jeff Davis corridor. Baptism by fire into police work running one call after another in the dark of night. Not exactly the seedy side of town, but far removed from suburbia.

Four years later as Becky and I were expecting our second child, I transitioned into the DARE, Drug Abuse Resistance Education, program at school. I spent five years learning the many facets of the public school system and presenting drug abuse prevention strategies to youth.

Hankering for a change, I went back to the streets, until there was an opening for a school resource officer (SRO) at one of the high schools. Moving into this role returned me to a normal schedule and afforded evenings and weekends at home. I spent three years gaining up-close and personal knowledge of the challenges, stresses and influences facing teenagers.

During that time, I was promoted to detective which led to my becoming part of the Crimes Against Children Unit. I would primarily work physical abuse and sexual abuse crimes against children. A year into this challenging role, my electronics and computer background led to being asked to investigate child pornography cases within the county. Shortly into my new role, I launched a program of stealthily finding and tracking online child predators, opening the door to my current fascination, computer forensics. A local FBI agent took me under his wing and sent me to several exceptional computer forensics training courses.

I quickly gained a reputation for my skill at interrogation. Whether it was gaining the trust of a child or a perpetrator, I had a knack. This is not something someone chooses, it chooses them. That level of responsibility led to becoming the lead investigator on cases where the county or the commonwealth's attorney could not afford to drop the ball or lose. When presented with a high-profile case, I was their guy, the one they trusted to obtain the evidence capable of bringing a conviction. Each step moved me toward this immense responsibility, working behind the scenes to capture incarnate evil.

CHAPTER 12

It was a gorgeous spring day in early May and time to file another weekend in the excellent memories folder and shift into Monday morning mode. Our band, Alibi, had played a gig on Saturday night. My days as a sax player enabled me to pick up the bass guitar and I joined a friend's band. Our blue jeans and t-shirt clad group comprised of five law enforcement officers who knew how to work hard and play harder. Whether it was band practice or playing a gig, our gatherings created the ideal outlet filling many weekends following taxing work weeks. A talented group of artists with an eclectic musical capacity that ranged from country to classic rock, classic blues to Motown. We could transport the parrot heads to the shore and even pull a few Beatles and Elvis hits out of our playbook. For two decades we performed in local restaurants, bars, and nightclubs. We took the stage at festivals, county fairs and summer celebrations all around the region. For years this was my primary, creative outlet allowing me to turn from the darkness into something life-giving and enjoyable. If the crowd was slow to fill the dance floor, our ladies would get the party started. I never drank alcohol and managed to embrace the party atmosphere without the need to become inebriated. Becky and I had a blast Saturday evening. The crowd responded enthusiastically and needed no prodding to fill the dance floor from the first song through the encore.

~

I paused outside the headquarters and enjoyed the warm start to the day. Co-workers were lingering in the courtyard. Some were catching up with friends from other departments, a few were taking a smoke break. My son, Mark had an early evening baseball game, and I promised to be there on time. I hoped clear skies and warm temperatures would linger through next weekend and set the stage for our first-of-the-season camping adventure. It had been a long, frigid winter. The landscape was awakening as the grayish brown of winter surrendered to spring. Everyone seemed energized even when facing the work week.

I was training a detective new to the Crimes Against Children Unit. Although each member of the team takes part in some aspect of training, new hires are primarily assigned to a more experienced detective. Detective Smith would be shadowing me for the next few weeks. I had been impressed by the instincts and perspective she shared during morning briefings. I was hopeful about her prospects with the team. Keen insight and fresh eyes reviewing our cases reminded us long-timers how intriguing the unit was when we first came on board. We all agreed that it would not take long for her to assimilate with the team. We also understood that few new members commit to the role for long.

I was actively juggling several assignments at various levels of intensity and activity. The nature of investigating requires flexibility, adaptability, and patience during the complex process. New cases were assigned weekly, and at a moment's notice required immediate reprioritization and seamless integration into our caseload.

I stopped to brief my sergeant, then sat down to check voice mail and e-mail. When the morning presented a rare lull of activity, I suggested Detective Smith and I drive to social services to get her acclimated with the office and staff.

I introduced her to several social workers and program managers we work cases with. Our impromptu visit was interrupted when the supervisor stepped out of her office. "Hey Rick, I just got a call from Ms. Miller, the counselor at Southside Elementary school. They have requested immediate assistance to investigate a serious child abuse complaint. They need an officer to meet with one of their students. A 10-year-old was brought to her office by a teacher, and they suspect she has a broken arm. The child's account of what happened was extremely disconcerting, and her mother did not call or send a note."

I motioned to Detective Smith, and we excused ourselves, thanked them and headed out. The timeliness of the call provided an excellent opportunity for Detective Smith to see the complex nature of negotiating trust with a young victim, an essential tool in this field. During our brief drive to school, I reminded her that although she would primarily be observing, her input was invaluable, and her observations crucial. I had no idea how significant and consuming this case would become for myself and the child.

~

When an unmarked police car arrives at school, and a plain clothes officer with a sidearm enters the building, conclusions are easily drawn. I tucked away the anticipation of my son's ballgame later that afternoon. I can still recall entering the long corridor. The cadence of our footsteps amplified by the hollow space. We entered the head office to subtle glances and the hushed muttering of staff.

We were greeted warmly by the principal, Mrs. Jackson, who escorted us to her office. "Detectives, thank you for responding so quickly. The student we are concerned about is Shantay Hunter. She is in fifth grade and has been a student here since kindergarten. Shantay is with the student counselor, Ms. Miller, in her office. They are expecting you. I spoke with the school nurse after she examined Shantay's arm. She does not believe her arm is broken, but it is quite swollen and there is considerable bruising. The nurse recommends her arm be x-rayed, to be sure. She is concerned that mom had not taken her in to see the doctor before sending her to school. Shantay said this happened over the weekend. Her arm has been placed in a temporary sling to minimize movement."

Mrs. Jackson patted a large folder on her desk with both hands. I could see several sticky notes protruding from the side, and Shantay Hunter's name typed on the label. "This is the student's folder. I am currently reviewing it, front to back, and finding any pertinent information. I will have my assistant make copies, including her attendance records and information from teachers from prior years that may be of interest.

"I also spoke with Ms. Tyler, Shantay's teacher. She will be collecting everything she has and is anxious to cooperate. She asked if you might be able to return tomorrow. She would like a face-to-face meeting and feels you may have questions that prompt things she has not considered. "Unfortunately, she has a classroom full of kids and no aide to take over. Please know, we have had concerns in the past but until now it has been speculative. Historically, we lacked concrete evidence. I hope this additional information validates our suspicions.

"Detective Meadows, Shantay has an older sister, Anita. She attended school with Shantay until approximately two years ago. I remember quite a bit because the staff was devastated. I want to be exact, so I have requested her file from storage. I recall Mrs. Hunter telling us that Anita had fallen at home and sustained a traumatic brain injury. Anita eventually returned to school but not here. There is a nearby elementary school equipped to serve severely disabled children. After her fall, Anita was profoundly physically incapacitated and could no longer communicate. She would be brought into school on a bed that resembled a gurney. I spoke with the principal of that school and visited her when she returned. It was shocking to see her decline.

"I was told that she typically sleeps much of the day, in part because of her anti-seizure medications. One morning staff had made several attempts to awaken her, but she was unresponsive. When they noticed her breathing had become very shallow, and her skin was cold and clammy to the touch, they called paramedics. She never returned to school. When Mrs. Hunter was notified, that Anita was being transported by rescue squad in critical condition, she responded defensively, saying Anita had fallen out of her wheelchair, but she was unaware of any injuries. It is my understanding that Anita now lives in a group home for disabled children outside the area. I have expedited my request for her records to be brought from storage. I will have copies ready by the morning."

CHAPTER 13

It the weeks that followed Mr. and Mrs. Hunter taking Anita and Shantay into their home as foster children, Mrs. Hunter's resentment toward the girls was obvious. Within days of entering into a pre-adoption agreement, Anita, two months shy of her sixth birthday, became a household servant for Mrs. Hunter.

Mrs. Hunter piled on the chores Anita was expected to do. Mrs. Hunter would inspect Anita's work which she used to rationalize her increasing excuse to discipline. It was not long before Mrs. Hunter unleashed fury upon Anita for no rhyme or reason. The litany of chores increased over the months, and before school began that fall, Anita was cleaning the bathroom every morning. Every Monday, Wednesday, and Friday she was responsible for dusting, vacuuming the entire house and mopping the kitchen floor. When the boys reported to Mrs. Hunter that Anita and Shantay were spending time together after Anita's chores were completed, Mrs. Hunter added clearing the table after meals, rinsing the dishes, and filling the dishwasher. Anything to limit the girls spending time together.

During the school year, except for cleaning the bathroom, Anita's chores were relegated to after school. Every task was expected to be ready for inspection when Mrs. Hunter returned from work. With seven boys in the home, this often-required Anita to clean the bathroom again.

Before the following summer, and before her seventh birthday, Anita was shown how to do laundry for seven boys. This daunting assignment required Anita to use a step stool to reach the washing machine. It also devoured much of her weekend, leaving little time for play or sisterly bonding. Shantay would help her big sister dust, but she was forbidden to enter the kitchen. The laundry room was downstairs and out of sight, so Shantay spent her weekends beside Anita, learning to fold clothes. Neither loved the work, but they loved being together. While the boys were playing sports or swimming in the pool outside, the girls sat together on the floor in the laundry room playing "go-fish" or "slap jack" waiting for the washer and dryer cycles to finish. Anything they could do together made life bearable. Sometimes Anita would pretend to read a book and the girls would tell secrets.

~

The adoptions were finalized and Anita understood no one was coming to rescue them. As Mrs. Hunter's beatings became harsher, Anita got tougher. She was determined not to cry in front of Mrs. Hunter. This seemed to incite Mrs. Hunter, and the after-school inspections often resulted in welts and open gashes from thrashings. It wasn't long before forms of punishment deviated to thrusting Anita's head against the wall or the edge of the sink in the bathroom. The look in Mrs. Hunter's eyes was pure evil when she grabbed Anita by the hair and slammed her head against any firm surface within reach. Anita began having severe headaches that left her dizzy and in bed early.

When the new school year began, Anita, now seven, was happy that she and Shantay would have a special time together once again. The bus ride to and from school was their only chance to be away from Mrs. Hunter and the chores that filled Anita's time. The boys walked to the rear of the bus, and the girls would sit together in the front. Shantay, now six, would help her sister in the afternoon and she had learned how to clean the bathroom as well as her sister.

Not long after school began, Anita was feeling upbeat and singing while she was cleaning the bathroom, which aggravated Mrs. Hunter. When asked, Anita's simple explanation of being happy to be back in school and liking her new teacher infuriated Mrs. Hunter. As Anita presented the bathroom for inspection, she smiled at Mrs. Hunter.

With an extra bounce in her step, she put on her jacket, and zipped her backpack.

Anita's chipper mood was met with contempt. When Mrs. Hunter began hollering in a familiar elevated tone it always led to punishment. Anita ran into the bathroom as fast as she could. Mrs. Hunter claimed she had missed a spot behind the toilet and forced the child to her hands and knees. She began railing, calling her stupid and pushing her nose to the floor telling her she better get every single spot or else.

Shantay had been standing in the living room waiting for her sister; her backpack strapped on. She could hear Mrs. Hunter screaming, and so did the boys who hurried out the front door toward the bus stop. Shantay was frightened and walked to the bedroom where Anita left her backpack on their bed, hoping her sister would fix what made momma so mad so they could get to the bus.

But instead of Mrs. Hunter being satisfied with Anita's rework, she slammed the bathroom door and the berating continued. Anita begged Mrs. Hunter not to pull her hair so hard and pleaded for her not to bang her head. Mrs. Hunter yelled all the time but something about her fury frightened Shantay. She covered her ears and began to cry, paralyzed by fear. Even with her ears covered, she heard the tremendous thump followed by silence. Anita was no longer crying, and Mrs. Hunter stopped yelling.

When Mrs. Hunter opened the bathroom door, crossed the hall and entered the bedroom where Mr. Hunter was, Shantay stepped into the hallway hoping to see her sister walk out of the bathroom. The silence was more terrifying than the screaming.

Shantay jumped when Mr. and Mrs. Hunter came out of their bedroom. Without a word, Mrs. Hunter opened the bathroom door and told Mr. Hunter she had fallen and would not get up. Shantay wanted to call for Anita. She wanted to run to the bathroom and see her sister, but she just stood in the hall paralyzed.

When Mrs. Hunter saw Shantay standing there, she chased her out the front door.

Shantay didn't think the school day would ever end. She spent the day on the verge of tears with her stomach in knots. She had never ridden the school bus without her sister. The bus ride seemed so loud with all the students talking at once. Shantay felt alone and afraid.

When the school bus dropped off the kids, the boys ran ahead. Mrs. Hunter's car was in the driveway and Shantay didn't know what to expect. She ran to catch up, hoping to see Anita. Instead, Mrs. Hunter sat everyone down and told them that Anita got hurt this morning, burned herself on scalding hot water and then fell down. Anita was in the hospital, but she won't wake up. She looked right at Shantay and told her she better not ask any questions. Then she told the boys that discipline is between her and the girls and no one else's business. She made each boy say, yes ma'am. Then they went outside to play.

Shantay was confused and sad. She did not understand what had happened or why she couldn't ask to see Anita. She curled up in the bed and cried herself to sleep.

When Anita returned home, they brought her in a chair that had wheels and laid flat like a bed. Anita could not move, not even her eyes, and she never spoke again. The days that followed Anita's return to the home were shocking. Shantay was beside herself with grief and confusion. She had to sleep in the bunk alone, and Anita was left in the living room by herself. Shantay had been forbidden to ask questions and the boys acted like Anita was not even there.

Mrs. Hunter immediately complained about having to put liquid in Anita's feeding tube and having to change her diapers. The reclining chair/bed was bulky and stuck out no matter where they set it.

Sometimes they stuck her in the corner facing the wall and would ignore her for hours. Mrs. Hunter fed her less and less and rarely removed her from the chair, leaving Anita soaked with urine until someone complained about the smell. When Mrs. Hunter bathed Anita, she wore thick rubber gloves, and the water would be so hot it steamed. When Mrs. hunter was in a particularly foul mood, she would pour boiling hot water in a dishpan and soak Anita's feet. The child was later seen with 2nd degree burns, a broken arm, and several other unexplained injuries.

When the "accident" was reported to the school, Anita was officially transferred to a local elementary school uniquely designed to assist children with profound disabilities. Basically, it was a resource that provided working parents with a respite. A large, specialized bus picked up children throughout the county. Anita would be wheeled to the van and secured for transport, taken to a classroom, and cared for during the day by trained aides.

In Anita's absence, Shantay, having just turned six, stepped into indentured servitude, Mrs. Hunter her unremitting taskmaster. Shantay was now expected to manage the chores her sister had been responsible for, except she was forbidden to enter the kitchen. While Mrs. Hunter continued to abuse Anita, Shantay had become Mrs. Hunter's primary outlet for revenge, which only escalated.

The same month Anita experienced her traumatic brain injury Shantay was treated for the first laceration to her forehead that required stitches. During that visit to the doctor's office Mrs. Hunter reported the incident as the result of Shantay's clumsiness and propensity to self-injury. Various concerns and reports were filed over the next two and a half years that irrefutably indicated Mrs. Hunter's continued abuse of Anita and escalating abuse of Shantay.

CHAPTER 14

The door to the counselor's office was ajar. A young girl was sitting at a round table with her back toward the door. Her hair was braided in rows with colorful plastic barrettes clipped at the end of each braid. A box of crayons and a half-colored page were on the table.

Ms. Miller was facing the child and in view of the partially opened door. When she saw us, she told Shantay that we had arrived. I introduced Detective Smith as a new member of our team, and stated she was with me to observe. Ms. Miller told Shantay that she was stepping out of the office and would be back soon. A quick scan of the space revealed Ms. Miller had created a soothing space for anxious children. A bowl of fidget toys was in the center of the table, an easy reach for tactile adults and children. The blinds were partially closed for privacy, but light was filtering through.

I knelt beside Shantay, introduced myself and waited for her to look up. "Good morning, Shantay. My name is Detective Meadows, and this is Detective Smith," I said motioning to my teammate. "It is nice to meet you. Do you mind if I sit down?" She nodded affirmatively and faintly smiled. She was subdued, her shoulders curved inward, her eyes fixed downward. Her arms folded over herself. She had not been crying, nor did she seem frightened. I relaxed my posture and leaned forward, easing into conversation. "I see you used purple and blue crayons in the picture. Are those your favorite colors?"

She shrugged. "Am I in trouble? I do not know what I did. Is momma going to be mad at me?"

"No Shantay, you are not in trouble. Your teacher and Ms. Miller are concerned about you, and your hurt arm. I would like to ask you a few questions. You do not have to be afraid to tell me the truth. Do you understand?" She nodded and looked up briefly.

"How old are you Shantay?"

"I'm nine, but my birthday is this summer and I will be 10," she offered with a bit more enthusiasm. "When is your birthday?" I asked. "It is in August. Momma already said there are no birthday parties for bad girls like me."

"August, that is my birthday too. That means you are a strong and brave Leo. Like Leo the Lion." I added, encouraged to establish a personal connection.

"No one ever called me brave. Why do you think I am brave?" she asked maintaining eye contact.

"I can see it in your eyes. You want to tell me the truth, but you are afraid of what will happen. Shantay, you can tell me anything, and I promise you will not get in trouble. I need you to use all your Leo the Lion courage to answer some questions. Can you do that for me?" I asked knowing she was up for the challenge.

Her body language softened immediately. Her self-protective arms unfolded and rested on the arms of the chair. I studied the features of her face. She had several large and jagged scars. There was a wide unhealed scar just above her left eyebrow and a larger one across her forehead. There was a deep wound from her upper lip to the bottom of her nostril and an older scar on her chin. Her earlobes were torn through from their pierced earring holes to the bottom of her ears. Most of the wounds had not been stitched, stapled, or even pulled together with a butterfly bandage. Her left eye was noticeably clouded, swollen and half-shut. She squinted from behind her large-framed glasses.

Her frail frame was swallowed by two oversized sweatshirts. Her shoes were worn out, scuffed, and stained. The shoestrings were filthy, knotted, and the ends frayed. Her big toes were bulging as if shoved into shoes too small for her feet.

83

When I asked if she would show me her arm, she used her right arm to carefully lift the other from the sling. Then she tentatively lifted the sleeve to expose her wrist and forearm. I understood the urgency of the call. I noted the widespread discoloration from bruising and the distorted shape of her swollen arm.

"That looks very painful. I am so sorry. Thank you for showing me. Can you tell me what happened?"

"I got caught sneaking food. Momma did not give me dinner Saturday night or breakfast Sunday morning. I knew I would be in big trouble if I got caught, but I was so hungry. One of my brothers had been eating a pack of peanut butter crackers. They went outside to play, and he left two crackers in the pack sitting on the pool table. I thought he would forget about them. I was scared but took them when no one was looking. Then I hid in the utility room where I sleep and ate them. When he came back inside, he started yelling about who ate his crackers. Momma must have guessed it was me. She did not even ask. She yelled for me to come upstairs. She already had the big stick in her hand. She grabbed my face and squeezed it hard and told me to open my mouth. When she saw food in my teeth, she swung the long board, but I put my arm up so she did not hit my face. That made her madder. She started hollering and swinging the long board all crazy. I tried to cover my head with both arms, and she whacked that arm again. She said I must be stupid, and something is wrong with me. Then she put the stick back under the couch and told me to go to bed."

Shantay seemed to forget that Detective Smith was behind her, fully engrossed in describing her home life. Her head lifted and eye contact increased. She seemed emboldened and began answering questions and offering details before I asked. She itemized the weapons they used to punish her and where they stored them for easy access with alarming specificity. Mrs. Hunter was the primary perpetrator, but

Mr. Hunter obviously colluded, tolerated, and never protected the child.

"Momma screams a lot and says mean things. One time she said, 'You cannot go to the store with me because your face is so ugly, I do not want to be seen with you. You stink too, go wash your butt.' Except she only lets me use cold water, so I take a very quick shower. I wear the same clothes a lot, and I am not allowed to wash them every week when I am washing my brother's clothes."

She described a black switch with a curly metal wire that came from a broken motor scooter. "The wire is sharp and tears my skin when momma whips me with it. Sometimes it gets stuck in my hair and momma yanks it hard until it pulls my hair out," she said. Then she leaned over to show me a recent gash between the braids in her hair. Her home-life was a war zone, and she a lone soldier surviving physical and emotional famine. She was a defenseless target besieged by rage and vindictiveness. Her mother's jeers poured out like salt on her wounds. Even rest was overshadowed by fear and pain, and sleep disrupted by nightmares.

"One day daddy came back from the store with a bottle of ammonia. He took the ammonia into the bathroom and shut the door. When he came out, he had my green eye drop bottle in his hand too. Instead of it being in the medicine cabinet, he put it under the couch. When momma started using the drops in my eyes, I could smell ammonia. The drops stung and burned so bad I shut my eyes tight and tried to get away. Then she started smacking my legs. I couldn't help it. When I knew the drops were coming, I could not be still. Then she started asking daddy to hold my arms and face. He forces my eye open. I cannot read the chalkboard anymore. My eyes are blurry all the time. It started looking worse than before and I try to close my eye. The kids make fun of me."

Shantay went on to describe her chores. "I clean the bathroom with bleach every morning before school. I got in trouble one day when the teacher called momma and said she needed to bring different clothes because mine smelled like bleach. I had a spill when cleaning that morning and got splatters on my clothes. Mom was so mad she kept me home from school the rest of the week. Now momma makes me clean barefooted, and I can only wear my panties. The bleach burns my skin and I get blisters on my feet. Want to see?" she asked.

Before I could respond, she slipped off one of her shoes and pulled off the dirty threadbare sock. The sole and sides of her foot were covered with blisters, some engorged and ready to pop, others open and inflamed; raw flesh, perpetually exposed directly to bleach, with no chance to heal. Honestly, I do not know how the child put on shoes or kept walking.

Her countenance slowly transitioned from shame and timidity to animation. She became fully engaged as she confided in me. How many people had she tried to tell this story to? She could sense that I believed her, and it emboldened her. A floodgate opened and unimaginable stories poured forth.

After one of her brothers began wetting the bed and ruined his mattress, she had to give up hers. For some time, she had been sleeping on the cold concrete floor in the utility room, next to the furnace. Her bed was a discarded blue and white barefoot shaped rubber bathmat. "At night there is no light. It is dark, and sometimes I get scared. Momma said if I need to go potty before morning, I am not to use the boy's bathroom or turn on a light. She gave me a big plastic bucket to go in. In the morning I take it outside and dump it way in the back yard and hang my rubber mat across the fence."

"Momma buys my clothes and shoes from thrift stores, and everything goes in a plastic box in the hallway. I am not allowed to touch food or any dishes. Momma says I am diseased, so I don't go in the kitchen. For dinner I get a sandwich, but sometimes just crackers and water. When I have cereal, momma puts water in it. Sometimes I am hungry when I go to school, and I sneak food from lunchboxes. All the boys eat breakfast and lunch at school, and they take snacks, but I don't.''

"I have an older sister, Anita, but she got hurt and she did not talk or walk anymore. She lived with us after but then she moved away. I did not get to say goodbye or see her again. I miss her all the time, and now I sleep alone, and I eat alone and have no one to play with or read to me.''

The unrelenting cruelty and bizarre forms of torture seemed far-fetched. But this was by no means childish exaggeration or attention seeking. Her adoptive mother was a deranged animal. When our conversation began, she was searching for something she could not articulate. Rescue. Shantay had opened the floodgates fearlessly. Shantay knew I believed her. For the first time in her life, she risked trusting someone with her only possession; the burden of her secrets. The only fitting response was to receive the gift and take the weight she had carried alone. I had every intention of earning the right to deserve that trust. As we finished the interview, I paused and leaned forward looking directly at Shantay with a smile. "I am so proud of you. Thank you for sharing with me. Now you know what brave feels like. I want you to remember that. Now a case worker is going to take you to the hospital and a doctor will make sure your arm is okay. I want you to be just as brave when she asks you questions, okay?''

CHAPTER 15

I opened the counselor's door and motioned for Ms. Miller. Jami Robinson had arrived from social services to escort Shantay to the hospital. Jami was an exceptional social worker and my favorite partner to work cases with. I knew Shantay would be well cared for.

Mrs. Jackson advised me that Mrs. Hunter had arrived and was in a small conference room out of view. The only window in that room faced outdoors. I confirmed that my intention is to seek immediate removal from the home. Mrs. Jackson asked if I could return in the morning to meet with Ms. Tyler and pick up the school records. I agreed.

I walked toward Ms. Robinson. "Jami, always good to see you. Ms. Miller will introduce you to Shantay. She is expecting to be escorted to the hospital. Shantay has been extremely cooperative, and her statements were compelling. I am seeking immediate removal and need an emergency foster care placement by this afternoon. If you can, research options for a stable long-term therapeutic placement as well. That is my goal. She needs the best we can find. I will contact forensics and have a technician meet you at the hospital for photographs. The child's mother is here, and I will be interviewing her next. Let me know what the doctor says."

~

I was confident the conversation would end with her arrest. Shantay's statement was consistent and thorough. In one accelerated leap, the case moved from suspicion to grave concern, immediate and long-term. I quickly reviewed my notes and jotted down key points for my interview with Mrs. Hunter. I was prepared to ensure Shantay would never be returned to her adoptive parents' house.

Interrogating an accused offender requires a different method of interview skills, yet both aim to build trust and elicit truth. I took a few moments to mentally transition and prepare to confront the bully responsible for demoralizing the sweet young girl I spent the last hour and a half with. The woman in the conference room waiting to spin a web of lies was a cagey, immoral character who had effectively deceived and manipulated countless agency professionals.

I have a fine-tuned internal lie detector which serves me well when confronting bullies who rely on strength and positions of authority to mistreat victims. My instincts for discerning falsehood were developed through countless hours of questioning abusers, pedophiles, and pathological liars. For better or worse, increased expertise led to being assigned as lead agent during high-stake, controversial, or high-profile cases. When investigations put a spotlight on the department and not the accused, they turned to me to get the job done.

Spring boarding into the bowels of society to snatch the innocent from the murky shadows is not for the faint of heart. The warped realities to which police officers and those working crimes against children are exposed to inevitably seep into the subconscious invading sleep and making unscheduled intrusions into everyday life. It forces the growth of thick skin for self-preservation. Eventually, I realized my belief in the goodness of humanity had been irrevocably damaged.

The first interrogation with a suspect can set the tone for the rest of the investigation. As I prepared to engage a suspect, I reminded myself that I was exactly where I was supposed to be; for such a time as this. Exposing nefarious behavior is not a skill of which one boasts. At some level, I hoped it did not somehow reflect a personal flaw that enabled me to get into their heads. When I wanted to quit and began discussing reassignment, I would take a few days off. Typically, after playing a few gigs, spending quality time with my family recharged me enough to return to the battle. I needed to remind myself what I was fighting for.

My gut told me there was no doubt as to the guilt of the mother, but I had to force myself to go in with an open mind, however I was convinced Shantay's statements were true. I was anxious to write up the affidavit for a search warrant and get on with collecting the evidence. I knew this woman had gotten away with her behaviors for some time. That was about to end. Mrs. Hunter was a pathological liar and manipulator, with a brazen sense of invincibility. This vindictive tyrant was about to be dethroned.

I knocked on the conference room door and without waiting for a response, opened it and stepped in. "Good morning Mrs. Hunter, my name is Detective Meadows." Her arms were crossed over her chest. Her hands tightly fisted ready to punch. She was a tall heavy woman, clearly accustomed to intimidating others. She was dressed in blue scrubs. She mumbled something under her breath without acknowledging my introduction.

"How long is this supposed to take? I need to get back to work," she blurted insolently.

I wondered how often that damning glare and those steely eyes had drilled through Shantay. I immediately sensed she could be beastly and believed herself to be above the law.

"You know that girl has been nothing but trouble since the day I brought her home. She and her sister both. She is a liar just like her sister was. They are both sassy and disrespectful, lazy, and ungrateful for a home. Shantay fusses about something all the time. She makes up stories acting like she is in some make-believe world. I cannot leave the child alone or she is smacking herself in the head. There is something wrong with that girl."

Mrs. Hunter was delusional. She either believed Shantay was too afraid to talk, or that I, like the others, could be persuaded to dismiss the child's claims. I think her abrasive demeanor would frighten most people. I sensed she knew and used it as an offensive or defensive tool to maintain control.

"Ma'am, do you know why the school asked you to come in today? Do you understand why I am here?"

"I guess that child's been lying again. What story is she telling now? I did nothing."

"Ma'am, did you notice that Shantay's arm is bruised and extremely swollen? Can you tell me what happened?"

"She must have hit her own arm this morning before school to get attention. Her big sister Anita taught her to do that. Both girls bang their heads on the bathroom sink."

"Mrs. Hunter, according to the school notes they contacted you last week concerned about Shantay's arm. During that conversation you told staff that Shantay had fallen while on the trampoline and that her arm fell through the springs where the mat is missing. Which one is true?"

"Well excuse me. I mixed up my stories. She fell last week, and her arm went through the springs. Like I told them, it looked fine to me. I told that girl not to play on the trampoline, and she snuck out anyway. If she just obeyed me, she would not get hurt all the time. The Bible says obey your parents, don't it? Serves her right for disobeying me."

"Why didn't you take her to the doctor?"

"Did you listen to what I just said?" she asked glibly. "It was not swollen and there were no bruises."

"Mrs. Hunter, tell me about the long stick with tape wrapped on one end?"

"What stick? I do not know anything about any stick. Whatever that girl is saying is a lie. I never hit that girl. I never hit her sister. I have never used a stick or nothing like that to punish her. Is that what she told you? After all I have done for her. Taking them girls in when I already had a house full of boys. This is the thanks I get for feeding and taking care of them after their own momma and daddy gave them away."

"Ma'am, have you ever whipped Shantay with a motor-scooter cable that has a curly wire protruding from the end?"

She returned eye contact and held it defiantly. Clinching her teeth, she barked, "I do not know nothing about that. Keep on asking me, but I said what I said."

"Mrs. Hunter, Shantay has several sizable and deep scars on her face. Some needed medical attention that was obviously not provided. Can you explain how she sustained any of those injuries?"

"Like I told you before, the child bangs her head, her arms, and her legs. She throws herself against walls, down on the floor, against the bathroom sink. Plus, she is clumsy, tripping over her shoestrings all the time. Look mister, I got seven boys, a husband, and a job plus that girl to look after. Do you think I remember every little thing that happens to one child? When my boys scrape their knee or fall off their bike they get right back up and keep going. She needs to toughen up. The world ain't fair and I am not going to kiss her booboos like she is a baby. She is so ungrateful. I had to leave my job to come on down here. Now my hours will be short on my paycheck. I mean no disrespect, but I got bills to pay and boys to feed and I cannot do that wasting time here. I need to go back to work. You keep asking me the same question a different way, but my answer is not going to change. Are we done yet?"

Unfazed by her contempt, I continued. "To be clear, are you stating that you have no recollection of how Shantay was injured or what occurred when she hurt her upper lip, above her eyebrow, across her forehead or on her chin?"

"Detective Meadows, what I do know is that the minute I take my eyes off her, she is getting into something. She's hurting herself or somebody else. That's why my boys do not like her and never play with her. This makes no sense. Why is she doing this to me? The girl has mental problems; she hears voices and says she wants to die. Does that sound like someone thinking right, someone you should believe more than me?"

"Mrs. Hunter, does Shantay clean the bathroom with bleach every morning, barefooted and wearing only underwear?"

"Every kid does chores. What about it? Yes, she cleans the bathroom. And that child ruined her clothes spilling bleach. I told her she will not get more clothes because she ruined what she had. Those girls were a mess when I got them. And now I am dealing with this. Doctors keep trying to get her straight, but nothing works. I can hardly keep track of all her pills. She takes more than an old man. She got two different pills for her being hyper, she is taking something because she is depressed, something else for fretting all the time. There is a pill for herpes too and pills for allergies and something I give her every day for an upset tummy. I think that girl has been stealing medicine and taking extra when I am not looking. I even told the doctor, and she said I better start counting them."

"And what about the eye drops?" I asked. Mrs. Hunter never flinched.

"What about them? Everything I give her the doctor told me to use or wrote a prescription for. There are pills, an ointment, and two different drops. She got herpes in her left eye from when she was a baby."

Her rehearsed lies were memorized and well worn. Obviously used many times before when she asked about her adoptive children's welfare.

"Mrs. Hunter, Shantay said she saw her father bring home a bottle of ammonia and then go into the bathroom. When he came out, he had an eye drops bottle in his hand. Instead of putting it on the counter with her other medications he slipped it under the couch. She said that since that time she can smell ammonia when you administer them. She said the drops burn and she begs you to stop. Would you like to respond?"

"The drops don't smell. I use what the doctor told me even though it does not work. Her eye is still nasty, and no one wants to look at her."

"Ma'am did Shantay begin to struggle and resist when you administered the eye drops? Did she tell you that the drops burned her eyes?"

"She never liked it when I put them drops in."

"Mrs. Hunter, did your daughter tell you that the eye drops burned, and that they smelled like ammonia? Did you start physically restraining her and using them anyway, after she begged you to stop? Did you ever smell the eye drops to make sure there was nothing wrong with them or check to see if they had expired? Did you contact the pharmacy or the doctor and report that your daughter was experiencing considerable pain when you used them? If we went to your house right now and smelled every bottle of eye drops in the home, would any smell like ammonia?"

"If there anything there that smells like ammonia, I don't know nothing about it. She is trying to accuse me of things I did not do. I do not understand why she is doing this to me. I ain't even been mad at her and we had a good week."

Mrs. Hunter was cornered and beginning to realize it. I was the first adult to challenge her fabricated excuses. I believed her daughter instead of her. I stood up and reached for my handcuffs. "Mrs. Hunter, you are under arrest for child endangerment. You have the right to remain silent. Anything you say can and will be used against you in a court of law. You have the right to speak to an attorney, and to have an attorney present during any questioning. Do you understand your rights?"

CHAPTER 16

As I drove from the school, back to the office to obtain a search warrant for the Hunter's home, I felt awash with shame. I have listened to hundreds of traumatized children describe their abuse, yet the abuse Shantay described permeated every single element of life. She had never known a safe adult that protected or provided for her. The only family she has is a sister, devastatingly taken from her by violence. Every opportunity to feel special or celebrated had been spoiled and she had worked more chores in the past two years than I worked my first eighteen years.

I thought about my own childhood, the adults who have sacrificed so much for me and my brother. How much they have loved us and provided us every opportunity to enjoy the simplicity of childhood and a limitless future.

The inconvenience that stuck in my craw, that I still recount as something the closest semblance of feeling "lack" was having to drink instant skim milk. Store bought milk was a luxury my parents chose not to afford, and it bothered me. Even worse was the rare occasion, when the tall red and white box of non-fat dehydrated powder was empty, our mom served diluted evaporated milk. True story; to this day that smell makes me gag. How petty that seems right now. Shantay had only been given water for her cereal and she never drank milk. My worst was better than anything she had known.

I remembered the weeks I spent at my grandparents' farm and how unnerving it was for me to wander through the darkness to use their outhouse at night. It was not as humiliating or as scary as Shantay being forced to use the bathroom in the dark, and into a plastic bucket.

Shantay's list of chores is inconceivable. Chores were part of my childhood, but my parents refused to allow chores to be the bookends of our day. Feeding grandpa's hounds was the only daily responsibility I ever had. I was about Shantay's age when it became my responsibility to haul the wood or coal in for heat during the winter. And I was prone to complain about it. Even when my brother and I were older, we shared the responsibility of mowing the grass in summer. And when we were old enough to drive, we only worked paying jobs during summer break. I had the benefit of parents that wanted their children to excel in school. And they sacrificially supported our pursuit of athletics, providing a healthy outlet for our physical energy.

Shantay had never experienced something as simple as a birthday. She had never been celebrated. My childhood memories are filled with mom preparing the meal of our choice every birthday and baking us birthday cakes from scratch. As simple as those moments were, I cannot remember a birthday mom did not indulge me by fixing and serving my personal favorite, chicken & dumplings with fresh corn on the cob.

Shantay had been starved, denied food served to the rest of her family. She was frequently sent to bed weak with hunger. As strapped as my parents were when we were kids, we had food a plenty. In fact, our day centered around the family meal. When the summer rains cooperated, and our garden flourished, mom canned the surplus of vegetables and fruits. Some years, her stockpile filled the makeshift shelves in the underground cellar. Mason jars were lined from end to end with enough green beans, corn, tomatoes, potatoes, and beets to last until the following summer. We never went hungry, never went without a hearty meal.

I have never taken my family for granted, yet I have only known a childhood of shelter, love and needs being met. It is impossible to imagine how different my life would be otherwise. My parents worked hard to ensure our needs were met, without complaining or focusing on what we lacked. I am convinced those humble beginnings increased my capacity for compassion.

CHAPTER 17

With a search warrant issued by the magistrate, I notified forensics that I was on my way to the Hunter's residence and confirmed their ETA. Detective Smith would ride with them and meet me there.

The family lived in an older, middle-class neighborhood, a few miles from headquarters. As I approached the house, I parked my vehicle across the street a few houses down. The home was a nondescript, suburban tri-level with signs of age but no obvious disrepair. The home was situated on an average size lot with homes on either side in proximity. It was hard to imagine neighbors had not noticed unusual behavior or overheard yelling. The Hunter's front yard was surrounded by a chain-link fence. The smell of freshly cut grass and the lawnmower sitting precariously in the middle of the front yard indicated Mr. Hunter had been interrupted from yard work. Trimmed boxwoods grew next to the front steps.

The forensics team was on scene awaiting my arrival. They had spoken to a neighbor who approached them after noticing the unusual activity at his neighbor's house. We can use forced entry, but we avoid unnecessary property damage when possible. Mr. Hunter offered the key, and the team prepared to enter.

Every member of the forensics unit plays a key role in extracting clues and supporting the integrity of information gathered. Objects that are identified as evidence are properly seized to preserve residual DNA evidence. Forensics technicians are highly trained professionals and have a meticulous process they follow like a script. One of the techs began taking photographs of the property as soon as she arrived. Once the constraints of the search warrant were understood by all, we entered the home. A search warrant would be explicit and correspond with the victim's testimony during her interview. It specifies which rooms can be searched and can limit such things as rummaging through every dresser drawer and reading personal mail.

The techs and I would continue through the house, searching separate areas and calling attention to the others as pertinent items were found. Items would be gathered and sealed in a tamper-proof container, chronicling the evidence along the way. One tech remained with me and took photographs as I documented where evidence was found. Upon completion of the first evidence gathering, if necessary, I would direct her to utilize a body fluid light or to dust for prints.

I advised Detective Smith that the magistrate had set bail and that I expected Mrs. Hunter to be released shortly. I asked her to watch for their arrival. If they insisted on coming indoors, they were required to remain in the kitchen during the search. She was to advise them that they were not to touch or remove any items or leave the kitchen until released to do so. I asked her to remain in their presence and pay careful attention to any conversation between them, but not to engage, ask or answer any questions.

We entered the tri-level and stepped into the small foyer. The aroma of bleach was immediately noticeable. Steps to the left led upward into the main living area. We would begin our search there. The steps to the right descended to the lower level. The utility room where she slept was downstairs. The home was sufficiently furnished, modestly decorated and surprisingly in order. This was notably one of the cleanest homes I had been in. The living room carpet looked freshly vacuumed. Scattered area rugs were all straight and the uncarpeted floors appeared mopped. There was minimal clutter, especially in the main living area. I thought it was remarkable considering it housed ten people, including seven school aged boys.

I walked toward the overstuffed two-tone gold couch in the living room. Decorative pillows were spaced evenly apart from one end to the other. Next to the large couch was a matching love seat, with coordinating pillows. As I approached the couch, hesitating momentarily before lifting the side to view any contents underneath. Shantay described exactly where we would find the objects used for her punishment. Quick, easy access to a storehouse of weapons used on only one child felt strangely out of place given the surroundings. The other children must have witnessed the abuse.

Stashed beneath the furniture was a bizarre, cryptic arsenal. Benign items amid random debris including a remote, a pencil, a sock, and several coins. Just as described, we found a 3 foot long, 1 inch thick, and 1 ¼ inch wide piece of lumber with the jagged edge wrapped several times with clear tape; a small green bottle with a "Refresh Tears" label, with contents that smelled like ammonia; and two black cords taped together at one end, with a metal coil wire protruding from the other with strands of hair tangled on the ends. Irrefutable evidence.

Our attention shifted to the dining area and kitchen. A line of prescription bottles was stacked on the shelf between the two rooms. Eleven labels were found with Shantay's name on the prescriptions. All were filled at the same pharmacy. Medications were out in the open contradicting Mrs. Hunter's concern about Shantay abusing them. Through the kitchen door was my first glance at the back yard. The deck showed the most age. The wood was weathered, paint chipping and several boards were popping up. The trampoline and above ground pool were in view.

We returned to the hallway toward the bedrooms. Straight back sitting in front of a linen closet was a blue plastic storage bin exactly as described. The 12 by 24 inches and 12 inches deep box held the sum of Shantay's wardrobe. The items worn but smelled fresh like detergent. Some of the socks and panties had holes or torn elastic. We found no other girls' clothing or personal items during the rest of our search.

When I opened the bathroom door, the odor of bleach burned my nostrils. The space was spotless, but I wondered how anyone could breathe in that noxious smell and have direct exposure to that poison through their flesh every day?

There were two bedrooms upstairs and two downstairs. The door to the boy's bedroom upstairs proudly displayed awards and certificates. The room housed two sets of bunk beds with only three mattresses. Superhero comforters neatly covered each bed. Every inch of wall space was filled with rows of storage bins. Each was packed with toys and games. Each storage bin rested on a long row of plastic drawers. The boys stacked games and books so high they could easily have tipped. Anything a boy would desire was within reach. The shelf in the boy's closet served as an overflow for toy cars and trucks next to a heaping assortment of winter hats and gloves. An array of jackets and winter coats filled the breadth of the closet. The closet floor was covered with shoes. During the entire search we found no toys specifically for a female child.

The parents' bedroom across the hall was a stark contrast from the order in the rest of the home. The upheaval seemed out of place. The dilapidated laminate dresser was strewn with junk. There were drawers missing where Mr. & Mrs. Hunter stuffed random items. Framed photos were sitting in chronological order on the top shelf of an entertainment center. Noticeably missing from the collection were photos of Shantay and Anita. Clothing and towels littered the floor. Stacks of paperwork covered with dust sat beneath dishes crusted with food. The closet floor looked like a massive hamper, with mountains of clothing waist high.

We made our way to the lower level. The rec room was framed – wall to wall with colorful bins, as they were in the upstairs bedroom. Each bin was overloaded with monster trucks, Tonka trucks, sports equipment, robots, dinosaurs, and every toy imaginable for boys of every age. Large sports themed posters hung throughout the room. Some were in cheap frames; others were tacked to the paneling. The longest wall in the room displayed a collage of family photos. There were family portraits, annual school photos and one for each boy for every sport and year they played. This grouping included a few of Shantay and Anita. Only one family photo included the girls. They were dressed in matching Christmas sweaters, their first Christmas with the family.

In the corner was an older TV, VCR, and rows of videos. The shelves above the TV and the mantle above the fireplace were lined with dozens of blue and gold sports trophies and team pictures in cardboard frames. On the other side, by the fireplace was an air hockey game and across from that was a pool table. Shelves held WWE character figures and equipment for video gaming. The storage area was cramped with scooters, skateboards, helmets, rollerblades, a bench press, a stack of weights, and a punching bag. Shantay mentioned being excluded from play. The favoritism was blatant, the disparity cruel. While the boys indulged in an endless array of activities and hobbies she was bound to a schedule of chores. The whole thing was pretty messed up.

The bedrooms were to the left. One was for the older boys. It had only two mattresses on the floor, with navy blue comforters pulled neatly over. Another older TV sitting on a small dresser was attached to a video game. A workout bench was in the corner. The second bedroom had two twin-sized beds with red comforters. Like the bedrooms upstairs, every inch of space that was not taken by furniture was filled with stacks of games and toys. More team trophies and photos were displayed on a long shelf below the window.

I returned to the open space and toward a doorframe with a makeshift curtain. I pulled the old sheet to the side. The floor was bare concrete. With my flashlight as the only light, I inspected the space. Old copper pipes were exposed between unfinished framing, no insulation or drywall. The hot water heater was aged and rusted. The front panel of the furnace was removed and leaning against the wall. The socket in the ceiling had a bulb but the string to pull the light had been cut to ensure Shantay was consumed by darkness. That cold and filthy, unforgiving concrete floor is where Shantay slept.

I pictured her frail, malnourished, scar riddled body curled in the fetal position, shivering from cold and pain. Her lip quivering as she lost the battle to fight back the tears. I felt nauseous and forced myself back to the sterile assignment of investigating. I channeled every ounce of professionalism into building a solid case. This madness had to end. How many times had she cried herself to sleep? How many prayers had she whispered in the darkness? How many nights had hate-filled words echoed in the silence? How many nights had she gone to bed hungry and writhing in pain with another gaping wound? How many times had she been awakened by throbbing pain from the blisters on her feet? This hellish place they banished her to each night was a condemning reminder that she was trapped, alone and abandoned.

My thoughts drifted to the times I tucked my children in their bed. There were many opportunities missed while working nights. The responsibility and joy fell to my wife who kept a consistent routine in my absence. I treasured the nights I was home to participate. I pictured my daughter's room when she was younger. I saw her pink princess bedding on a canopy bed and heard childlike prayers. I would kiss her forehead and wrap her blankets tightly. My children knew the immeasurable love of a mom and dad who adored them and each other. My heart sank, and for a moment my composure with it. I never grew accustomed to the shock and repulsion of it all. Nothing about this becomes normal. I despised the gritty underbelly of the work I did. I loathed the exposure to depravity because it made me suspicious and cynical. There was no immunity.

We exited through the basement and into the back yard. There was an above ground pool surrounded by an aluminum deck. The trampoline was beside the pool with a net encircling it and the protective mat intact, covering the springs. There was a heaping pile of plastic toys next to another overflowing toy box. An older, rusty swing set was beyond that. The shed, near the rear of the yard, had a hole in the roof and a piece of green plastic carpet nailed over the exterior of the rear window. The wooden floor had a few holes where the ground below could be seen. It held various outdoor tools, a mower, some bikes, and a ladder. Behind the shed, straight back to the fence I saw the white plastic bucket on the ground beneath a blue and white foot-shaped rubber mat draped across the chain-link fence. In the far corner, there was an area where something had been dumped over time killing the grass.

We found everything exactly as she described it.

CHAPTER 18

By the time I was back at my desk, the timer on my watch beeped its first countdown to leaving for the ball field. My son's enthusiasm for sports was invigorating and reminded me of my own youthful endeavors. I had given my word that I would attend every game barring an emergency.

I had also given everything I had today for what I believed would change the trajectory of a young victim's life. Several agencies had successfully collaborated. The cyclical quest for justice often resembled a disjointed two steps forward and three steps back. Today was a banner day with no steps back.

My job dedication bowed to honoring my commitment to my son. It gave me permission to shift from detective to dad. The sun was setting on a taxing workday. Time to compartmentalize the trauma I had seen and heard. I trusted Jami had found a suitable placement and helped her settle in.

I thought this case would meld into the collective sorrow of a hundred others. There was considerable work to be done before the weekend. I adjusted my schedule for the rest of the week. Forensics will have the photos taken at the hospital by morning. Jami and I will talk about prioritizing and coordinating strategy. I had no idea as I drove my car and shifted my thoughts toward my beloved family, that Shantay would become much more than just another child victim rescued from domestic violence and abuse.

~

At the end of the workday, I crossed the threshold of my home and flipped the switch. I protected my family from the heart-wrenching details of the cases I worked on. Not merely because of confidentiality, but because they deserved a husband and father attentive and engaged in the life we were creating. I tucked the burdens of the day neatly below the surface and turned my focus to them. They were my unrivaled priority. My family needed me to live out that commitment in practical ways. That was my grandpa's legacy and my goal.

I strolled toward the baseball field. It was the second inning; and Mark's team had a 2 – 0 lead. They were enjoying the home team advantage with bleachers filled with exuberant fans. I spotted my son standing near the dugout with his teammates. He is tall, lean, and handsome. He had become quite the ballplayer and was excelling as their shortstop. Watching him in his element was pure joy.

I scanned the sea of fans, and it did not take long to find her. Becky would arrive early and reserve seats in the same familiar section. She and I had developed a routine for managing the kids' activities, balancing my unpredictable schedule and our robust calendar of activities. The moment I saw her I smiled, and much of the tension of the day fell away. Lord knows, I love this woman. I protect my family from the lurid details of my day job. Truth be told, it is their love and her stability that protect me. My marriage and family kept me from spiraling downward and losing myself to the disturbing realities to which I was exposed. When I was quiet and needed to lean on her, she offered shelter.

Becky is the anchor that keeps our family stable, just like my mother was in our family. She keeps me grounded. When frustration and stress invade my carefully compartmentalized life, when my laid back demeanor turns snippy and impatient, she learned to give me space. I took a moment to watch her. Becky is my favorite person in the world. She still has long blonde hair, just like the day we met. She is a soft-spoken and gentle beauty. She has a kind soul and a quiet strength that fortifies me. She is virtuous and optimistic. Her soothing presence purifies me. I could not subject myself to the horrors of the job if it were not for her. Becky is the most genuine person I know. Her unassuming demeanor welcomes others and sets them at ease.

She has never met a stranger and is typically chatting with someone by the time I join her on the bleachers. The intensity of the day dissipates when she kisses me hello. She learned to interpret my moods with instincts developed through years of experience, the way I learned to read a perpetrator. She senses when I am still sorting through the day and need time to unwind.

I have watched the job chew up and spit out decent men and women. The pressure, the evil, and toxic stress wreak havoc. This type of work is mentally and emotionally fatiguing. Half the battle is a legal system that feels like it works against us. Those not wise enough to disengage and pro-actively support a healthy home life can get sucked into the undertow. Without intentionally investing in regular healthy outlets, unguarded men and women slip into drinking and indulging in self-destructive or immoral behaviors to escape.

We are blessed with two amazing kids. Holly and Mark thrive in their respective grades and enjoy friendships and various social activities. Somehow, they still enjoyed spending time with me and their mom. We knew this time was fleeting and wanted to capture every moment of their youth and bottle it. Our children's lives were fairly idyllic when compared to the lives of the child victims I worked with. The contrast could be disconcerting, yet it brought needed balance. I needed to remember the world can be a good and hopeful place.

I lived for the weekend, not because I did not love my job. In fact, I was pretty darn good at what I did. Making a difference was important to me. I know Grandpa would have been proud to know that I developed a 95% successful confession rate that drew respect from my peers and acknowledgment of leadership. Still, my absolute best day pales in comparison to the life we were building as a family.

There was such an ease to our marriage. Even during challenging seasons, it never felt impossible. Perhaps because we married so young, but we learned to face obstacles turning toward each other.

Leaving or giving up has never been a consideration. She is my favorite place to be, and I am hers. No matter how successful our separate lives were, time together was preeminent. Regardless of how adventuresome our hobbies were, the best part about them was mutual interest and the camaraderie we shared. Friendship first. We worked together to build a marriage that incorporated fun, music, friendships, and simple adventure. Unlike many couples, our favorite activity was whatever we were doing together.

Our children grew up believing that quality time was a natural element of family life. They were sheltered but in the healthiest way. When sports were not in full swing, weekends included band practice and playing bass and singing backup vocals as a member of the band Alibi. There were many weekends that Becky and I were gone more than home. They always say working out is the most beneficial activity for stress, but that is the tip of the iceberg.

Weekend plans were fashioned around the kids' activities. With an unusual weekend free, we were looking forward to camping again. Springs were spent at the baseball field and autumn at various sporting events watching our daughter Holly cheer. Summers were given to camping as often as possible. We would pack up and head to the mountains or travel to West Virginia to visit family or to visit my brother.

~

Becky noticed me watching her from beside the bleachers. She smiled brightly and motioned for me to join her.

It was no surprise when the team won by a landslide. We took the kids out for a late celebratory dinner. As we waited for our pizza and talked about our camping adventure, I gazed with awe at my children. Mark's face, still smeared with dust, was beaming. His sister, as beautiful as her mom, was laughing aloud about something my wife said. In that moment, all was right in our world.

Just over Holly's shoulder a young girl walked by. She was petite with hair braided in rows with barrettes on the end of each braid. Shantay's face flashed across my mind and gripped my heart. The laughter in front of me faded as I wondered how she was. She would be settled into a temporary foster care home, in bed for the night. Oh God, is she okay? Does she feel safe or is she wide awake, frightened, uncertain, or sad?

Meandering thoughts were quickly interrupted by piping hot pizza being set on the table. I reached for a hefty slice and thanked my lucky stars for the love around that table.

CHAPTER 19

I drove straight to the elementary school Tuesday morning. I arrived prior to my meeting scheduled with Ms. Tyler to review the documents that had been copied. Mrs. Jackson handed me a thick manila envelope with school records then led me to the conference room. Clipped together in the front were various notes from former teachers in sequential order. Three distinct handwritings chronicled concerns and pinpointed dates that began the timeline. Anita's records were clipped separately.

Ms. Tyler thanked me for returning to meet with her. She sat across the table but seemed hesitant to begin. Her eyes were tearing up.

"Detective Meadows, I need you to know how much I care for Shantay. I hate what she has been going through, and I am so relieved it is finally being investigated. As I combined all my notes and various contacts with her mother and incidents just from the school year it was sickening. I did not sleep a wink last night."

"Ms. Tyler, I appreciate your honesty. I am not here to interrogate you or question your concern for the child. You made the call about her arm. That got the ball rolling. We can focus on that. Tell me what you know and have seen firsthand."

Before she opened the folder, she began sharing.

"I thought I was doing everything within my power to help the child day by day. Mrs. Hunter was dismissive, curt, and intimidating by phone and in person. My approach to our communication, including offering positive feedback about Shantay's academics changed throughout the school year. I was more guarded and began documenting her responses in direct quotes. I have my handwritten notes with dates and her responses but not as detailed at the beginning of the year. I want to offer more than a list of facts; I want to share this information with the impact it had."

Ms. Tyler did not wait for me to respond and continued.

"Not long after school began, I found her crying in the bathroom. She said she was missing her sister, that they always rode the bus together. When I asked if she talked to her mom about how she feels she told me she was told never to mention Anita's name again. I was the only person she could talk to about her sister. During the first parent-teacher conference I asked Mrs. Hunter if she knew Shantay was desperately missing her sister. Had she considered taking Shantay to visit her or possibly arranging for counseling to help her process her feelings. Mrs. Hunter told me it was none of my business and threatened to pull her from my class if I ever spoke with her daughter about personal family matters again. From then on Shantay and I kept those conversations   between us.

"In late September she came to school with her upper lip split open. Not just cut, but a deep gash that caused a large amount of skin to hang and flop. It was disturbing and looked incredibly painful. The other children were staring, and she could not close her mouth or talk right. When I contacted Mrs. Hunter, her response was blasé. She said Shantay had been roughhousing and fell against the fireplace. When I told her that I was in the nurse's office and Shantay needed stitches, she was irate that she had to leave work. She expressed no sympathy for her daughter. The nurse later told me that Shantay waited in her office for well over an hour. But the next day her lip was stitched. Honestly, I do not know how long that gash had been there, but it never healed properly even with stitches. Shantay refused to say what happened.

"By the end of the first grading period, it was clear that Shantay's ability was just below grade level. She did not have an IEP, and it was unclear why she was in my LD class. I told Mrs. Hunter that she could easily integrate into a few mainstream classes, she would enjoy P.E, music, and recess. I thought this would be encouraging. Her response astonished me. She became combative and launched into a

112

tirade about her daughter being emotionally disturbed and how she needed to be 'contained.' She accused me of challenging her parental authority and asked if I thought I knew her daughter better than she did.

"I did not agree that her restrictions served the child's best interest. It is challenging to have a child in the room all day with no breaks. Initially I was annoyed, in fact I resented it. I was stuck with a student all day. But it did not take long to realize that Shantay was no trouble at all. She enjoyed helping with simple tasks like erasing the chalkboard. Many days she laid her head down and slept during recess.

"It is peculiar that she always dresses in oversized, layered clothing. She wears long sleeves and long pants no matter what temperature it is. At first, I thought she was cold natured because she is slender. But even when it is very warm outside, she wears the same few outfits. Mrs. Hunter did not allow Shantay to eat the free school breakfast or lunch even though the family was eligible. When I checked, I discovered her brothers eat school meals every day. She is my only student that is not supplied a snack. Mrs. Hunter claims Shantay suffers from stomach issues and requires a strict diet.

"One afternoon during recess while she was sleeping, I stepped into the hall to speak with another teacher. When I returned, I found Shantay digging through the trash. When I asked what she was looking for, she said a classmate had thrown away half their sandwich and an apple, and she had not eaten. She confided that her mom often denied food as punishment. When she ate dinner most of the time it was a sandwich, sometimes only crackers. It seemed absurd but she looked thinner and seemed weak. Between you and me, I started bringing snacks every day for her to eat during recess, until today."

After several minutes of recounting details, Ms. Tyler stopped speaking. She stared at the unopened folder she brought and sighed.

She drew a tissue from the pocket of her jacket and dabbed her nose. She tried to continue but her voice cracked. She covered her face with both hands and began to sob. "I don't know why I didn't do more. I saw the signs every day. I found her digging through the trash. I knew she was wearing the same few clothes. I looked at her thinning face and listened to her grief-stricken stories about missing her sister. I saw every wound that we contacted her mother to address. Teachers are told what to look out for and I just took notes. I should have done more. Why did I think bringing a snack and letting her sleep during the day was enough? Detective Meadows, I am so sorry. I failed her."

"Ms. Tyler, you did what you believed was right. I would imagine you were concerned that Mrs. Hunter would insist Shantay be removed from your class. Who is to say another teacher would have brought her a snack, let her sleep or taken the time to listen to her. Those kindnesses mattered and Shantay will remember them. Based on that folder, it looks like you have taken excellent notes. That detailed documentation will become vital evidence to support this case. Your commitment to capture those details is evidence we would not have otherwise. You made the call today. You pushed for action today. You have my word that I will see this through. It might help to focus on that."

She nodded her head and looked up. "Thank you, Detective. Forgive me for blubbering. This is not professional, I apologize. I love my job; I love being a teacher and I care about my students. But when I put all this documentation together it was overwhelming." Ms. Tyler opened the folder. "I typed up a list by dates and made copies of the documentation which I have included for you."

"I contacted Mrs. Hunter on several occasions, but I highlighted where the concerns were urgent. I already mentioned her lip. That was in late September. It was the worst, but not the first. She was out the second week of school. When she returned, she had what I can only describe as a "bleach stain" under her left eye.

"In late January she came to school on a Friday reeking of bleach. Her fingernails were yellow, and her fingertips were covered with sores. Her sweatshirt was covered with bleach splatters, some spots were damp. Shantay felt nauseated and had a severe headache. I asked her mother to bring a change of clothes as soon as possible, but she was unable to leave work. The nurse found suitable clothing in lost and found but Shantay was afraid to change saying she would get in trouble. When the nurse convinced her that it would ease her headache and she could keep the extra clothes, she conceded. But she refused to undress in front of the nurse. I verified my notes. Shantay was absent until the following Tuesday. The next time we were alone she told me her mother had forced her to stay outside all day and clean the backyard.

"She also came to school with the skin on her ear ripped and she never wore earrings again. She would not discuss what happened. There was also an injury to her chin, a deep cut that was not stitched and no explanation was provided. I did not document when, but both were this year. The cut on her chin may have been there when she returned from Christmas break. When she returned from spring break, she had a significant cut over her eyebrow and on her lip. Whenever I asked Mrs. Hunter about Shantay's injuries, she quickly defended herself and reiterated that she is violent and self-injures. I have never seen her show those behaviors toward others or herself. Detective Meadows, Shantay even told me that she sleeps on the floor in the basement on a rubber mat and uses a bucket as a toilet at night. She takes so many medications, it all seemed so far-fetched."

~

I thanked Mrs. Tyler for her honesty and thorough notes and drove back to the office. En route, thoughts of the stark contrast between Shantay's childhood experience and my own jabbed intrusively. I was livid for all she had been denied and grateful for the benefits that made our lives feel extraordinary. Family members who instilled confidence and parents who afforded opportunities for kids to identify and develop interests and pleasures in things, such as sports and music, that still influence my life today.

Mrs. Hunter ensured Shantay's school experience was a living hell, forcing her into isolation and classes that did not challenge her academic capacity. Mrs. Hunter filled Shantay's days with brutal labor and prevented the benefit of good sleep, nutrition, exercise, and friendships. She annihilated wonder and the exploration of hobbies and extracurricular interests. She denied even the basic benefits of participating in music, art, physical education, and recess with classmates.

Throughout our years in school our parents guarded afternoons and evenings, insisting me and my brother concentrate on our studies, complete our homework, and practice our sports. They encouraged us to participate in sports and activities. Harnessing our energy instilled characteristics that formed us and our careers.

CHAPTER 20

The evidence was compounding, and every detail substantiated Shantay's statement. Reviewing school records and aligning them with the details provided by her teacher, it was clear the abuse was acute, persistent, and pervasive. It was obvious she had done the same to Anita and gotten away with it. Detective Smith walked in with a cup of coffee in one hand and documents in the other. "Good morning, Rick. I typed up my observations during your interview with Shantay at school. I also captured various comments made by Mr. and Mrs. Hunter during the home search."

"Excellent, thanks. Jami Robinson will be here shortly to discuss what transpired at the hospital yesterday. I would like you to participate in the conversation. Would you mind checking with forensics and picking up the photos taken during her examination?"

Detective Smith returned with a bulky packet and set the envelope on my desk. "Thanks. Tell me about the Hunters? I understand they were rather chatty."

"Yes sir. They seemed agitated, especially Mrs. Hunter. They never stopped talking. They kept trying to explain themselves or maybe they were getting their stories straight. At times they seemed to be talking to each other, other times they directed their comments to me or one of the nearby techs. I did not engage. They repeatedly implied that she is prone to self-harm. Mrs. Hunter mentioned they had been through this two or three years ago when Shantay accused her of hitting her in the head with a baseball bat. It seemed odd that she would draw attention to that incident. Mrs. Hunter said Shantay made this wild story up because she got caught stealing candy from a convenience store. She knew she was in trouble and hurt her own arm to avoid punishment. Then Mrs. Hunter proceeded to demonstrate how Shantay could have slammed her arm before school. At times, Mrs. Hunter seemed antsy and would pace. Off the record sir, she reminded me of a caged animal. Mr. Hunter was more docile; not calm but reluctant. Mr. Hunter only responded to her promptings. Later in her ramblings she mentioned the incident with Shantay's arm, insisting that the child fell off the trampoline last week and that her arm looked fine. At one point they seemed to be talking back and forth, reiterating that Shantay cannot be left alone because the moment they turn their back she will self-injure and Mrs. Hunter even tried to demonstrate how Shantay would lean forward and strike her head on the bathroom sink, saying it was just like her sister Anita had done."

"Good work. Thanks for capturing that information. Send me those electronically and I will add both statements to my report. Mrs. Hunter is not accustomed to being challenged. A little pressure has her tripping over her lies. She has never been confronted about her ludicrous statements. Let's see how she handles being under the microscope"

About that time, Jami walked into my office. "Come in; good to see you. I think you met Detective Smith yesterday. She will be shadowing me on this case, and I have asked her to join us. I met with Ms. Tyler, Shantay's teacher this morning, and picked up her and Anita's school records from Mrs. Jackson. There is a lot coming together quickly. How was Shantay when you took her to the emergency foster care home?"

"Better than expected given the circumstances. Shantay was a trooper, at the hospital and later when I introduced her to Mrs. Thomas. Initially reluctant, but once she saw she would have her own room, her eyes lit up. Mrs. Thomas was about to prepare dinner and asked Shantay if she wanted to help. When I left, they were headed into the kitchen together."

"That is great. I thought about her last night. How was your trip to the hospital?"

"Shantay responded very well to a highly complex situation. She was nervous and unsure what to expect. It was a long afternoon, and we were there four hours. Sweet girl was worn out and slept through the drive back," Jami began.

"Four hours, that is a long time. Was that because you had to wait in the emergency room?" Detective Smith inquired.

"Great question Detective Smith," Jami responded "but no. If a citizen walked into the ER that might be the case, but when child protective services and the police department are involved, either the case worker or detective contacts the hospital in advance. They knew we were bringing her in and prepared accordingly. We are incredibly lucky, living in this area, to have direct access to the highly distinguished Medical Director of the Child Protection Team. She is one of the best, if not the best, Pediatric Emergency Medical and Child Abuse doctors in the state. She also has a dedicated group of certified trauma nurses trained to recognize abuse and collect evidence. We bypassed the ER and waiting area. As soon as we arrived, they led us to a secluded exam room. It wasn't long before a trauma nurse came in and advised us the doctor would be meeting with Shantay. That is not always the case if she is tied up with another patient. Whether it's the doctor or one of her trauma specialists, they will complete a comprehensive evaluation and provide a detailed report. The doctor is often called to testify as an expert witness in court, so either way she reviews all reports. I'm sure you will meet her and her team soon enough. Have you seen the photos?"

"We have them, but have not looked through them," I responded. "Detective Smith brought them moments before you arrived. Would you mind telling us about the afternoon, and share your insight as you show them to us? This is great training for Detective Smith," I said handing the envelope to Jami.

Jami and I worked child abuse cases in a reciprocal partnership built on a solid history. She was the only social worker I trusted implicitly. Her casework was impeccable, her integrity unquestionable, and her commitment and advocacy wholehearted.

Jami opened the sealed envelope and glanced through the contents. "From the moment the pediatrician entered the exam room she was empathetic and gentle with Shantay. This doctor is known for her uncanny ability to put children at ease. I have seen terrified children, unwilling to speak, trust her. She has a disarming bedside manner. Before she removed any part of the gown or touched her body, she explained what she was doing. The tech had taken a few photos before the doctor arrived. Shantay feigned a smile but seemed to feel exposed. Kudos to the tech who followed the doctor's lead and began asking before she took photos. Once Shantay's anxiety subsided, she no longer seemed frightened or reluctant.

"Before she helped Shantay onto the exam table, she had her stand as we partially removed the gown to examine her frame, front then back. The child is skin and bones. Her rib cage and hip bones, sternum, scapula, and clavicle are overly pronounced. It reminded me of those haunting images of concentration camp victims. Her flesh is riddled with lacerations, bruises, burns, blisters, scrapes, and scarring at every stage of healing. We took close-ups of each scar. It seems like Mrs. Hunter knew precisely how to inflict abuse without extinguishing her life," she said handing me selected photos before she continued.

"Shantay is suffering from severe malnutrition and anemia. The anemia is partly from lack of nutrition but exacerbated by blood loss from excessive bruising and some internal bleeding. Shantay has not gained weight in three years. The file included photos from an exam a few years ago. The scars now covering her body were not present at that time. After the exam, the doctor ordered bloodwork and an IV for dehydration. She ordered x-rays not just for her arm, but her leg, and spine too. She noted Shantay's responses were 'age appropriate, and her developmental level normal.' Before she left the exam room, she asked the nurse to arrange for a meal to be delivered as soon as possible. Shantay devoured every morsel and asked if she could have more. When that was brought in, she consumed every bite of that one too.

"Despite all she has endured, the doctor characterized her as 'alert, pleasant and cooperative.' She truly was. There is a light shining through and she seems hopeful. She was exhausted and napped during the drive back to my office.

"Now, let's talk about the scars, starting with these," she said handing me several. I studied a series of six photos zoomed in on two disturbing and distinctively shaped burns. One had a row of lines equally in distance, curved in an arch shape. The other scar was concentric. It looked like rings surrounding a larger, solid spot in the center.

"Rick, she knew exactly how they got there. She said her dad held a hot lightbulb in a rag, then pressed it into her chest sideways, held it there firmly and then rolled it. That arch shaped burn is the threads of a burning hot lightbulb. Then he pressed the socket end of the bulb into the other side of her chest and held it there. That burn created what looks like a bullseye."

I shook my head in disbelief. "You have got to be kidding me. It is as if he was intentionally branding her."

"Consistent with what she described to you, Rick, Shantay told the doctor she had not fallen from the trampoline, reporting her mother hit her several times with the big stick of wood. She also told the doctor that her mom hits her almost every day with the stick or whips her with a curly cable. She added that recently her mother bent her legs backwards and it made her limp."

Jami handed me the rest of the photos. "Rick there are twenty-two large or predominant scars."

"Unbelievable. I will contact Mrs. Thomas and arrange a second interview with Shantay. In the meantime, I have an idea. When the Hunters come in for their interview with CPS, I would like you to set some bait. I know you don't address the 'weapons' per se, but introduce the idea that we found blood on the stick. Mrs. Hunter vigorously denied using the stick, or any weapon, to discipline Shantay. Once she believes we have Shantay's DNA, she will contrive a story and coordinate their responses, which will contradict her prior statement."

"No problem. I will see them tomorrow. Rick, I'm not done. There is more."

CHAPTER 21

Jami retrieved a document from a file and continued. "I spent some time this morning researching the family's prior contact with CPS. There have been several complaints investigated. Some arose from concerns from school personnel, others were anonymous tips.

"There was a report filed when a neighbor called 9-1-1. The call came in after 10:00 p.m. and the caller reported 'the child had been outside for an extended period in cold weather.' The caller advised police that 'when she plays outside, she looks like she is scared and shaky.' He added that he 'always sees bruises all over her and that her parents make up reasons why and keep her covered up.'

"I also cross-referenced Anita's name and discovered something major. Rick, the evidence keeps coming. There is an unnerving déjà vu pattern of abuse, not only with her older sister, but with Shantay. The types of injuries and behaviors have been known and reported to multiple professionals for six years. Even Mrs. Hunter's excuses and blame shifting is a pattern. Legitimate concerns were raised, investigated, and confirmed by doctors prior to the adoption being legalized.

"I found an Affidavit for Emergency Removal Order for Shantay and combined ex parte preliminary protective order for Anita. This investigation followed Anita being transported by rescue squad from school in critical condition. The sworn statement was painstakingly researched. It is an exposé citing thirty-two recorded incidents or statements from individuals with first-hand knowledge of the children. Mrs. Hunter's history of reporting that both girls engage in self-injurious and suicidal behaviors, and display psychotic symptoms, were uncorroborated by several identified sources. Based on the overwhelming evidence, the social worker urgently requested an emergency removal order for Shantay. She further requested the court prohibit the Hunters from removing Anita from the group home where she was living and returning her to their home.

"The incriminating concerns of neglect and abuse, supported by evidence, mirror the current investigation. Rick, these concerns were presented three years ago, overseen by our office. The social worker did everything in her power to advocate and intervene. I cannot explain why those requests were denied.

"Their early history is missing. The report begins with the girls' birth names and the county where they had been living. Their parents lost custody when Shantay was four and Anita was five years old. There was a reference to possible sexual abuse, but nothing specifically stating why the parents' lost custody. Nor was there an explanation for why the Hunters agreed to foster them here, two hours away. The connection is not stated. Were they the children of a family member? A younger sibling or a cousin? Had someone blindly convinced decision makers that placing the children with 'family' no matter how distant or unhealthy, would be more advantageous than strangers? Why would any agency approve a pre-adoption order for two young girls to be placed with a family with seven boys when they could not provide separate sleeping quarters?

"The evidence reaches as far back as the early months after the Hunters became temporary foster parents after entering into a pre-adoptive agreement. The affidavit lists three separate complaints alleging nutrition concerns, an unexplained black eye, second degree burns requiring skin grafts on the older child's feet, other scratches, cuts, and reported beatings. These concerns were shared with the Department of Social Services in the Northern Virginia jurisdiction that had legal custody of the children. Yet they chose to relinquish their legal obligation to protect the girls, formalized the adoptions, and frankly, sealed their fate. What am I missing? Could the biological parents have requested the Hunter's become the girls' adop tive parents?

124

"Approximately four months after the adoption was finalized, Anita suffered the traumatic brain injury causing her to be permanently and profoundly physically handicapped with no language abilities. The injury was never reported to CPS at the time, and later Mrs. Hunter reported the injury resulted from a fall in the bathroom. According to Mrs. Hunter, prior to Anita's traumatic brain injury she attempted to drown herself, and deliberately rode her bicycle in front of a car attempting to take her own life.

"The child remained with the family two additional years, experiencing a series of ongoing injuries, documented by CPS and the school. These included a report of scratches to Anita's vaginal area. Again, Mrs. Hunter claimed self-injury and the child flailing her arms as the cause. An unfounded disposition of physical abuse was determined. While bound to a wheelchair, Anita continued to receive burns to her feet. There were other reports indicating vaginal bleeding had been observed on another occasion, as well as abrasions in her mouth and under her tongue and other unexplained injuries. Mrs. Hunter consistently claimed self-inflicted injuries as the cause, including head banging, aggressiveness, lying, and feigning and exaggerating illness. The school nurse also reported that Anita sustained a broken arm before Christmas break. It does not state if an explanation was provided.

"The final medical emergency occurred when Anita became unresponsive and school personnel called 9-1-1. It was noted that she also had abrasions to her lip and forehead. Admitted in critical condition, her CT scans revealed a 'subdural hematoma.' Mrs. Hunter later mentioned Anita had fallen from her wheelchair two days earlier, but she did not feel medical intervention was needed. She continued to report Anita's behavior as manipulative and problematic, yet the child had no ability to communicate and was essentially in a vegetative state.

"When bloodwork revealed that Anita was not receiving her anti-seizure medications, the explanation given was that it made her vomit. Based on hospital and school counselors, and CPS, it was finally agreed that it was not safe to return Anita to the Hunter's home. At Mrs. Hunter's insistence that all injuries were self-inflicted, the group home for severely disabled children rescinded admission acceptance. After a second interview two weeks later, Anita was transported directly to the facility by ambulance.

"Within the two months that followed, Anita gained ten pounds and staff noted only two startle seizures. That evidence resulted in a 'founded' disposition of the medical neglect and abuse allegation, and the formal Petition legally preventing the parents from removing her from the group home. But that is not all.

"During that time, reports alleging abuse on Shantay were received. Within two months of Anita being hospitalized and placed in a group home, CPS began receiving abuse allegations for Shantay. One family doctor mentioned treating Shantay on three occasions for head lacerations. The first incident was a few months after they became temporary foster parents. This doctor also reported having a high level of discomfort regarding the girl's overall welfare. Another doctor reported concerns about suspicious things which could not be proven. He went on to say the mother had her hands full prior to the adoptions, and the adoptions seemed to put mom over the edge.

"The injuries that Shantay was treated for include being seen at a local hospital for stitches in her forehead. The injury was reported by Mrs. Hunter as a fall in the bathroom. During that visit, the doctor found an older injury, a gash under her tongue 3 centimeters in size, an injury identical to one Anita had when she reportedly fell in the bathroom. Other reports during this time included the child being forced to stand with arms outstretched while holding weights for extended periods of time. This was corroborated by her brothers who were interviewed separately. The Hunter's sons reported that those things were between mother and child and not to be discussed by, or with, other family members.

"Mrs. Hunter used the same tactics, saying Shantay was prone to aggressiveness and self-injury, claimed the child hears voices, hallucinates, bangs her head, hits herself and others, and wants to die. After the psychiatrist at one of the hospitals supported Mrs. Hunter's concerns about self-injurious behaviors, and recommended admission for mental health observation, Mrs. Hunter refused to allow it. The same hospital had recorded Shantay being treated for two head injuries later that summer, both requiring stitches. Staff noted during each visit that the child was very pleasant, polite, delightful, and talkative.

"Shantay was admitted to a different pediatric psychiatric facility the following day and several days after, she was reported by staff as doing well.

"The affidavit states that school personnel showed she was doing very well. The teacher had never seen the extreme behaviors the mother indicated were happening at home. She noted Shantay reporting extreme food restrictions, sleep deprivation, and being forced to remain outside for extended periods of time. Shantay had been discovered going through garbage cans and searching for food.

"Despite that exhaustive account, a perplexing and egregious decision had been made refusing to act upon the social worker's concerns. Opinions and warnings backed by four physicians, school personnel, a babysitter, and the findings recorded during admission to a children's psychiatric facility, went unheeded."

"Jami, this additional information is sufficient evidence for me to file an added malicious wounding charge on Anita's behalf."

I turned to my computer and expanded the scope and range of potential police contact. I found a report corresponding with the timeline of the affidavit. It was written by the detective who visited Shantay at the emergency foster home where she stayed during the investigation three years prior.

According to the officer's notes, the child (Shantay) "seemed very capable of answering their questions." When asked if she understood why she was living in foster care, Shantay responded "because my mom hit me in the head with a baseball bat and it made a bump on my head." She went on to say, "the first time she hit me, I was just getting dressed and it was for no reason. It happened at least five times and she also struck me on my bottom and legs with a stick." The officer stated there were "no notable marks." The officer indicated that Shantay remembered the day her sister "fell in the bathroom," saying "Anita had spilled her milk and donuts in the kitchen and went upstairs to brush her teeth. Then she heard a fall in the bathroom." Shantay was told that Anita "had been burned by scalding water, passed out in the bathroom, and hit her head." The report also references a complaint being filed about the suspicious nature of Anita's second-degree burns. The detective's assessment of Shantay stated the child "skipped around a lot" to allow her to explain what was happening to her.

Good grief, the child was barely six years old. She was being terrorized and clearly traumatized. It is a wonder she answered as well as she did. I shook my head in disbelief. This evil began six years ago.

Detective Smith stood up and excused herself for an appointment.

"Detective Smith, before you leave, I want you to know that I appreciate your input from yesterday. It has been an intense two days. You have witnessed and heard very disturbing facts. The good news is there is copious evidence working in our favor. The chances for a positive outcome for the victim are improving by the hour. That will not always be the case. We are going to get this one right. I know it is a lot to process but focus on that."

When Detective Smith closed the door behind her, I sighed. I was grateful for a few minutes alone. "Jami, you know I am committed to every child victim we work with. But, I must admit, there is something special, something different, about this girl. We have both seen excessive child abuse. But this girl, her entire life has been a succession of multi-system failures not just once, but repeatedly and over several years. You cannot make this stuff up. Behind that frailty, is a warrior. I do not believe she would survive another failure. Nor do I believe it is an exaggeration to say her life depends on us getting this one right."

"Rick, it is no coincidence that this case fell into your hands. You are the right person for this case. I know how you operate. I will do my part from the CPS side and together we will protect her. For now, Shantay is safe and being cared for. Mrs. Thomas is a highly respected therapeutic foster parent. She has worked with children in temporary, emergency situations for years. I am working on a long-term placement to present to my supervisor. I cannot think of a better investigator to advocate for this girl. We have every base covered. We will wrap things up before you leave Thursday night. You can still take Friday off and enjoy your weekend. It will be good for you to get away. If anything comes up, I will be here to handle it."

CHAPTER 22

Jami and I met shortly after I joined the Crimes Against Children Taskforce. I had spoken with her occasionally as the school resource officer and when attending training facilitated by social services. When I moved into my investigative role, and began working exclusively with children, contact became frequent as we worked cases together. The time invested comparing and combining evidence forged a remarkable partnership. When she was assigned a new case, she chose to work with me and vice versa.

Jami was single and fifteen years younger than me. I became an older brother. As our relationship developed conversations drifted into our personal lives, family history, marriage, and dating. Her father was a highly respected police officer in a large, metropolitan region. Everyone knew him or knew of him; his reputation preceded him. Her first memories were of him in uniform. She grew up with her father working rotating 24-hour shifts. He was absent or sleeping more than he was present. Home life was different when he was there. Adjusting to his overbearing personality felt like a roller coaster she wanted to leap from. He was well respected in the community and admired among his peers, but swift with a backhand to keep order at home. He ruled his family like subordinates, expecting his children to fear, revere, and obey without question.

The secrecy and contradiction had affected her. She vowed never to date anyone in law enforcement, period. She assumed all police officers were hypocrites, playing hero at work and oppressive authoritarian at home. When she moved away, she wanted nothing to do with men in uniforms. The unresolved conflict with her father influenced her responses to potential suitors.

Jami is a lovely woman, educated, articulate and a relentless advocate for child victims. Despite her fierce resolution, she found herself inexplicably drawn to a younger version of the man who ruled her childhood. After college she moved toward social work and began working with victimized children. She was too invested in her passion to back pedal once she realized how often she had to work with police officers. The role forced her to associate with aggressive personalities, some of whom triggered her defenses. The success of cases required communicating and trusting a breed of professionals she preferred to avoid. She described working in partnership with me as a rose among thorns.

Single men on the force who knew we were friends would probe for information. Casually asking if she was dating. Even when she found herself attracted to someone, and intrigued when I mentioned his interest, she could not bring herself to reciprocate. She was no easy catch. Would be suitors did not stand a chance. Occasionally, she would meet a guy whose flirtation had piqued her interest. With persistence, and of course charm, she would concede and meet him for coffee or a drink. The more a guy bragged the less interested she became. More than a few first encounters were last encounters.

Many lunches were a combination of casework and coaxing her off the ledge of self-doubt over pizza and garlic knots. I tried to convince her that not all men, or police officers, were jerks. I had to admit, her experience had proven otherwise. I was delighted when Jami met a man who sparked her interest beyond anyone she had dated. A friend introduced her to a man from out of town. Like my introduction to Becky, the attraction was immediate and undeniable. She and I met for lunch one afternoon and from the moment I saw her she could not resist smiling. "What in the world is going on?" I asked.

"Rick, the man I met is incredible. I really like this guy. Besides being ridiculously handsome, he is charming and respectful. He seems like the real deal. I do not know how this happened. All the vows I made against dating a man in uniform. Then I meet the most decent man I have ever dated, and I find out that not only did he graduate from The Citadel, but he is in law enforcement. Now I am falling for a man who lives out of state, and his career is the field I swore I would never consider. You are an excellent judge of character, and I do not trust my blind spots. I want to bring him to the house; I want to introduce him to you and Becky."

For months he made the trek to visit Jami as often as he could. They would come to the house; I would cook out on the grill, and we played cards for hours on end. Watching them together sealed the deal. Not only did I approve, but I could not have chosen a more suitable man. When they tied the knot, and she relocated it was a tough goodbye. I was thrilled for them, but selfishly missed the rare professional connection we shared that helped me endure the nature of our mutual work.

On days like today, and countless others, I thanked my lucky stars for Jami Robinson. She and I spent years entering the arena fighting side-by-side in the war to rescue children. Iron sharpened iron and we combined intellect and perspectives to unravel mysteries and align strategies. There were times I wanted to explode, or worse, could have imploded. Jami and I became allies that understood how to handle conversations that revolved around disturbing topics such as sexual abuse, victim statements, shattered lives, hospitalization, mutilation, and even death. Today I felt responsible for Shantay's future. No one else could have understood it quite the same way.

For years the ability to vent behind closed doors was a sufficient outlet when balanced with the support of life off the job. Jami and I could discuss details that no human should be exposed to and left to process alone. Having a trusted comrade in the same battle kept us both from madness. After several years with the task force, I was more beat down than I realized. The responsibilities being added to my role, and the implied liability, had become unreasonable. I managed a revolving door of multiple cyber sting operations, while supervising staff also actively engaged in numerous stings. In addition, I was expected to be available for field operations and take on cases. I was excellent at my job, but this level of expectation was irrational. The pressure was horrendous, and the stress was burying me.

At the time the department offered no support to their detectives. The vision of peer support had not been conceived. Detectives in similar positions in other jurisdictions were being evaluated annually. They were required to meet with a psychiatrist to ensure they were coping. It reached a point that I openly volunteered that information to my supervisor, implying that I was struggling beneath the intensifying pressure. I waved a passive white flag that went unnoticed or unheeded.

I continued to function well at work, but the pressure built to boiling. My mind was saturated with information and my ability to compartmentalize felt like ten fingers plugging a levee with eleven holes. It became impossible to shake the day, frustration began spilling out at home. Instead of leaving the pressure behind, I shoved it into a massive backpack and carried the weight of it into my home. At its worst, I became ill tempered; my fuse was short and flared without provocation. My wife was struggling to understand the man she loved, unable to contain this uncharacteristic behavior. I refused to ask my wife and children to suffer the consequences of my two and a half decades of dedication to law enforcement, the last seven of which I spent surrounded by violence and perversion against children. I turned in my retirement papers a few months shy of twenty-five years.

CHAPTER 23

On my way to Mrs. Thomas's home to interview Shantay a second time, I made a quick detour to find a lion stuffed animal. Our shared birth month created a natural connection and a fun way to empower her. She had been exceptionally courageous and having "Leo the Lion" as a tangible reminder seemed perfect. I wanted to present it to her when I arrived for our second interview.

Shantay was looking out the living room window when I pulled up to the house. She waved. Before I could ring the bell, she opened the front door and said, "Hi, Detective Meadows, would you like to come in?"

"Hi Shantay," I said squatting to eye level with my hand behind my back. She reached for my neck and wrapped her arm that was not in a sling around it. The child is a fountain of resilience. "I am happy to see you again, and I brought you something. Do you remember we talked about our birthdays in August? August birthdays mean we are Leos, like Leo the Lion, brave and strong."

"Yes, I do remember. What is behind your back? Is it something for me?" she asked curiously.

It was the first time I had seen her smile. "Yes Shantay," I said offering her the cuddliest lion I could find. "I know you are a big girl, but if you ever feel sad or lonely, I want you to hug this Lion and remember how brave you are."

Mrs. Thomas smiled, extending her hand for me to shake, and welcoming me in. "I guess it is safe to say you are Detective Meadows? Hi, I am Mrs. Thomas, please come in," she said with a chuckle. "The living room is all yours. I collected my ironing to occupy myself and give you two some privacy. Cookies are in the oven, and I will bring some out a bit later."

"Thank you, Mrs. Thomas," I said turning my attention toward Shantay. "How are you today young lady? Did you sleep well last night?"

"It was nice sleeping in a bed, but it took a long time to fall asleep. Mrs. Thomas did not wake me up early or make me do chores. She cooked bacon and eggs for breakfast, and it was delicious! I have my own room. Do you want to see it?"

"I would love to," I responded mirroring her enthusiasm.

"I told Mrs. Thomas where I slept at momma's house, and that I wanted you to see my room. So, I know it is okay," she said taking my hand. We paused briefly at the opening to the kitchen. Mrs. Thomas was removing a sheet of cookies from the oven.

"Did Shantay tell you that we made dinner last night? She was a terrific helper."

"Oh, yes. I did help. We made chicken nuggets, French fries with ketchup, and green beans. When Mrs. Thomas asked me to set the table, I told her that momma said I was diseased and not allowed to touch the food or dishes. She told me not to worry about that. I just needed to wash my hands first, just like she does. It took longer because I could only carry one thing at a time, but when I finished setting the plates, napkins, silverware and glasses, I told her helping was fun, not like the chores momma makes me do."

I could not refrain from smiling at the joy she felt doing such mundane tasks; chores most children would complain about. Still anxious to show me her room, she pulled me to keep walking. When we reached the doorway to her room, she stopped, dropped my hand, and ran ahead. I was not sure what to expect. She stood in the middle of the room, then swung her arms wide and turned in a perfectly awkward pirouette.

"I have never had my own room and look how pretty it is. The bed is soooo soft and warm, and I have TWO pillows!"

She plopped herself down on a corduroy beanbag chair in a reading nook. A tall lamp in the corner arched over the space creating a circle of light above the chair. The small bookcase beside it had three shelves filled with books. "This is where I can read or have quiet time."

"What a great space," I said. "I love it!"

"I took a long hot bath last night. Mrs. Thomas poured bubble bath in the water. She told me if I moved my hands around fast that it would make bubbles, and it did. I stayed in the tub until my skin was all wrinkly."

Her smile faded just as quickly as it had appeared, and suddenly the girl carrying the weight of the world surfaced. "I felt sad last night. When Mrs. Thomas said goodnight, she put a nightlight next to my bed and showed me how to turn it off and on. I did not want her to think I was a baby, so I said no thank you. But after she closed the door, I switched it on. I was not scared of the dark. I kept thinking about how mad momma is going to be when I go home. She will punish me for telling everyone about my arm. When will they make me go back?"

"Shantay, I will work extremely hard to make sure the people who make those decisions know all the things you told me. I promise. I have questions I need to ask you about your visit to see the doctor. Let's go back into the living room."

Unopened bottles of water had been set on the end table and the coffee table. Mrs. Thomas stepped into the living room. "I will be back in the laundry room at the far end of the other hallway, if you need me."

"Thank you, ma'am."

"Shantay, tell me about your trip to the hospital."

She was quiet for a moment, her eyes far away. "When we got there, we walked down a long hallway that was all glass. That was just to get into the hospital. Then we took an escalator and then an elevator. When Ms. Jami told them who she was they took us right back to a room by ourselves.

"There was a gown folded up on the table. The nurse held it up and asked me to take off my shoes, my sweatpants, and my shirts. I did not have to take off my socks or my underwear. She asked Ms. Jami to help so I did not use my arm. The gown was so big it kept falling off my shoulders 'til Ms. Jami tied the strings in the back tighter. I was uncomfortable sitting in a big chair waiting for the doctor. I did not like being undressed and I was cold. The gown was so long it dragged on the floor. I was a little scared, but mostly I was cold and glad I had socks on. When Ms. Jami saw me shivering, she took a sheet and laid it across my lap. Then she opened the door and asked someone to bring me a blanket.

"I told Ms. Jami that I was not allowed to talk to a doctor. Whenever Momma takes me to the doctor, she makes up stories. She says I hurt myself, that I throw fits and act wild like an animal. She says I am clumsy and walk into walls, and trip over two left feet. When the doctor asks me a question, she answers. If I start to talk, she glares at me, and I know she will whip me. So, I stay quiet. She told them my brain does not work right and I do not understand enough to explain for myself. Why would she say such terrible things like that about me? Why did everyone believe her?

"At the hospital, the doctor looked right at me and asked questions. At first, I did not answer; I was scared I would get in trouble. Ms. Jami told me everything would be okay, and I could tell the doctor everything. She told me I was safe and that the doctor wanted to help me. She lifted me up on the table, so I didn't hurt my arm. She looked at my arm, moved it around, and squeezed a few places asking me if it hurt. Then she asked me to tell her what happened when my arm got hurt. Then the doctor looked all around my body asking me about bruises and things. I was nervous at first, but the doctor was nice. She told me everything she was doing so I was not scared. She even rubbed her hands together to make them warm before she pushed on my belly. Ms. Jami wrote things down and the other lady took pictures.

"The doctor told me my arm isn't broken, but she wanted to make sure.

"She told me she knew I was in pain, so Nurse Matthews was going to bring me something to help. She wrapped an ice pack in a towel and laid it on my arm. She said it would help with swelling, but it made me feel cold.

"Then she said, 'Nurse Matthews is going to take some blood. It may sting for a second. You can look away if that helps, but you need to be still. I am ordering an IV. Do you know what that is? Your body is dehydrated. That means it is thirsty, so we will give you some extra fluids. The nurse will put a small tube right there and tape it in place. When the plastic bag hanging on that hook is empty, they will take you for an x-ray. When you are all done and dressed again, Nurse Matthews will put your arm in a sling. For now, I want you to lean back on the pillow, while I lay the bed back just a little. Try and relax. If you are sleepy you can nap.' Then she covered me with a blanket and asked the nurse to have a meal brought to me. When they brought the tray in, I ate the whole thing and then asked if I could please have more."

~

A conversational style dialogue will prompt more natural responses than a series of leading questions. While that seems obvious, trust cannot be demanded, it must be earned. I watched as Shantay sank into the pillows that surrounded her. She curled her legs up close beside her body and leaned into a pillow she laid on the arm of the couch. Leo the Lion was sitting beside her. She pulled the crocheted Afghan from the back of the couch and laid it across her. During such lulls in conversation, she was subdued, just as Jami said she had been at the hospital. When Shantay began to share her countenance brightened. For years, her life dangled by the thinnest thread, and she coped by making herself small and unnoticeable.

"Shantay, tell me about what it was like at home. What was a typical school day like for you. And what do you do on weekends."

"It was my job to clean the house. Anita did most of the cleaning before she got hurt and was in a wheelchair. When that happened momma made me do the work. I clean the bathroom every morning before school. I told you about that the other day. One time she mixed ammonia and bleach together and made me clean the bathroom with that. It burned my eyes and my skin and my throat. I started coughing and could not stop. I threw up. She closed the door and it hurt to breathe. I heard dad fussing about how bad it stunk even with the door closed. She did not make me do it again. I had a bad headache all day and even the next day. I could not talk from my throat hurting.

"Momma wants the house neat when she gets home from work. When the bus drops us off, I put my backpack away. First thing I do is pick up the dining room and the living room while the boys do their homework and watch TV. On Saturdays I do all the laundry, except for momma's clothes. The boys take sheets off the bed, but I wash them and put them back on. That takes a long time.

"On Sunday I vacuum and dust. I am not allowed in the kitchen though. I wash my plastic bowl, cup, and plate in the big sink

139

downstairs in the laundry room. I cannot touch any dishes or food cause momma says I am 'diseased.' Sometimes the boys tease me saying I have 'cooties.' She said I have had it since I was born and that is why they put drops in my eyes. Since the drops started smelling like ammonia, my eye feels worse.

"I am not allowed to play with any of the toys or games or ride their bikes. Because I am diseased momma says I cannot go in the pool. Sometimes I watch them through the window and sometimes I sneak outside and hide where they can't see me when they play."

Then she paused, words hanging mid-air. "Sometimes momma takes the boys shopping, or they all go somewhere without me. Momma locks the doors and makes me stay outside. She tells me to use the bucket in the shed if I need to potty. Sometimes she did not let me back in at night, and I had to sleep in the shed. I do not like being in there. The bugs and spiders and holes in the floor make it creepy. When I saw her throw away an old blanket, I took it out of the trashcan and hid it in the shed. One time I was outside all day in the cold and the door was locked. A neighbor asked me what I was doing outside for so long. I did not answer him and ran to the shed. A police officer came to the backyard and another police officer was in the front talking to mom. They made her let me inside."

She did not speak for several minutes. We sat together in silence and bore the weight of grief that filled the void.

CHAPTER 24

Mrs. Thomas entered the living room carrying a tray with two frosty glasses of milk and a plate of chocolate chip cookies. "I thought you two might enjoy a snack, warm from the oven."

I watched Shantay take the first bite of the soft warm cookie. It folded gently and the melted chocolate oozed. She closed her eyes and smiled with wonder as if tasting such deliciousness for the first time. I felt the pangs of conviction for all the simple pleasures I take for granted. Shantay reminded me that our capacity to experience joy is proportionate to gratitude.

"These cookies are scrumpdillyicious," I said, lifting my glass of milk to hers. When our glasses clinked together, in unison, we said, "Cheers." The playful gesture was priceless.

~

As Shantay indulged in a cookie unafraid of her mother's wrath, I contemplated her life with a mother who intentionally denied her the simple pleasure of play and outdoor fun. Much of my youth was worry free and filled with enjoying the outdoors adventures with my grandpa and my brother. Our property was isolated from neighbors and me and my brother forged a bond that continues to this day. We had vivid imaginations as kids, and our memories are saturated with hours spent exploring the woods, building forts, swimming in the creek, and tossing the ball. I can't count the hours we spent fishing off the banks of our little stream, using corn and salmon eggs to catch trout. And when the seasons changed and our ventures led us to catch bass and catfish, we wandered through the woods to a lake. We brought worms and liver as bait, and mom would pack peanut butter and homemade jelly sandwiches, waving goodbye as we headed down the long dirt road. It was one of our well-worn paths. The only rules we had were to have fun, take care of each other, and be home before suppertime.

Shantay had not a single such memory in her storehouse. Her sister, the only one she had any positive memories of, was gone from her life. Her would-be brothers excluded her at every turn. The cruelty was unfathomable.

~

The serendipitous timing of our milk and cookie break seemed to lighten the heaviness. And I continued the interview.

"Shantay, I have the photos that were taken when you were at the hospital. I am going to show you some that she took of your scars, like the one on your chin. I need you to tell me everything you remember about what happened when you were hurt. If you do not remember everything, tell me what you do remember. Can you do that?"

The photographs had been divided and categorized. I glanced through the section I had pulled when preparing for this interview. There were twenty-two photos with prominent scars in various stages of healing. Some were deep and/or large traumatic injuries that should have been medically treated but appear to have not been. Photo #2 of #22 focused on a deep jagged scar just above her left eyebrow. This injury was documented by the school as a significant laceration that needed medical attention. They initiated contact with Mrs. Hunter requesting Shantay be seen by a physician.

"Can you tell me what happened here?"

"Momma hit me with the long stick. We were off school for a week in spring, around Easter. I have seven brothers; did I tell you that? They play sports in summer and during school. They ride bikes and skateboard around the neighborhood. When they play video games or air hockey or pool, they never let me play. It was warm outside, and they were playing football. Saturday is the day I do the boys' laundry. I had been washing, drying, and folding for a long time. All the clean clothes were stacked on the table. I filled the washing machine with stinky socks, t-shirts, and underwear.

"The window in the laundry room is way up high. I could not see anything, and I wanted to watch. The rule is no play or going outside until all my chores are done. I decided to sneak out just to watch. At first, I sat under the deck where the bikes are. Then I moved a little to feel the warm sunshine. Momma was upstairs in the kitchen fixing lunch. The boys did not know I was there, and I forgot she could see me. Suddenly she started banging on the window so loud I jumped. Then she lifted it up and started yelling, 'Girl, you better get your butt back in this house.'" I ran inside as fast as I could. When she came downstairs, she had the stick in her hand. 'How many times do I have to tell you the rules. Are you dumb?'

"I tried to tell her the clean clothes were folded, and I was just watching the boys while other clothes dried. She did not care, she was mad. I should not have run, but I did. She swung her arm stretching across the air hockey table and hit me so hard I fell and knocked my head on the corner. At first, I could not get up. I did not want her to hit me again. Blood was running down my face. She lifted the stick up again, but then saw all the blood and told me I better not get any on the rug and walked away. I pulled my shirt up cause it was bleeding a lot. She threw a rag at me and told me to wipe that mess off my face and get myself cleaned up before I touched the laundry again.

"The next morning was Easter. When the boys got their baskets with toys and candy, I had to stay downstairs. She did not take me to the doctor either. When I went back to school the teacher called her and asked what happened. She told them I hurt myself and refused to go to the doctor."

"I am so sorry Shantay. I know it is hard to remember and talk about these things. You are doing great." Then, I showed her photo #3 which focused on her left earlobe. "Can you tell me what happened to your ear?"

Her hand reached for her left earlobe. "One day after my shower I forgot my towel. I tip-toed to the hall closet to get one. Momma saw me in the hall with the towel wrapped around me, and my clothes on the bathroom floor. She thought I left them there. I ran into the bathroom to pick them up, but it was too late. She headed straight to the couch and grabbed the black cord with the curly wire. She was yelling for me to pick up my dirty clothes, but they were already in my arms. She started swinging and whipping me on my head and face. When I turned away, the wire part got caught in my hoop earring. She pulled a few times, but it did not come out. Then she yanked until it ripped my skin. The earring was still stuck in the wire and blood was dripping from my earlobe. She untangled the earring and threw it at me; "I guess you won't be wearing those again."

Reliving the memory provoked a visceral response; she winced and lifted her shoulder to her ear.

"Shantay, I'm so sorry that your mom has done such mean things to you."

"Do you promise they won't make me go home like they did before, like they did when my sister moved away?"

"I promise I will work extremely hard to prevent that. I know it makes you sad to talk about what happened. Sharing these terrible memories that you had to keep secret for so long will help me tell the judge how badly they treated you."

Next, I pulled out photos #6 and #7 and held both up. "I know you told the doctor that these are burns from a hot light bulb. Can you describe how that happened?"

"Daddy did those. One of my chores is to clean the bathroom with bleach before school. One morning the light burned out when I was cleaning. I opened the door and turned on the hallway light, but it did not help. I called out to daddy and asked if he could help me. When he finally answered he had a t-shirt in his hand. I asked if he would please change the light bulb. so I could finish cleaning. He was staring down and me but would not say anything. Then he reached up to the hallway light and with the T-shirt took out one of the bulbs. I thought he was going to use that. I backed away so he could get to the sink. Instead, he turned around and laid the burning hot light bulb. sideways into my chest and pushed it into my skin. I backed away until I hit the wall, but he kept holding it there. Then he twisted it like he was turning a knob. I screamed, 'Daddy, that burns. Please stop. What did I do wrong?'

"Daddy did not answer me or say anything. He put it back into the hall light and took out the other one with the T-shirt. 'Daddy, please don't burn me again. I'm sorry.' Then he took the light bulb. and pushed it into my skin on the other side of my chest with the round metal part that goes in the socket. He turned it round and round. I tried to stop crying but he covered my mouth with his hand. When my nose started running it dripped on him, and he let go. He never said a word to me. He wiped his hands on the t-shirt and walked away. I had to finish the bathroom in the dark with my skin burning. It hurt even worse when I put my shirt on."

What kind of monster thinks of such bizarre forms of cruelty? "Shantay, I am sad that he did that to you. He was not a good daddy. Daddies protect their little girls."

"When the eye drops started burning, I could not be still. I squeezed my eye shut and turned away. Momma made daddy hold my head and sometimes he would force my eye open. If I moved, he held my head still."

Shantay inhaled deeply and sighed, shrugging her shoulders. She became restless, adjusting herself, trying to get comfortable. "Do you have a lot more questions?"

I glanced up and smiled. She watched as I finished my notes. I knew this was a huge ask, but I was not done. This was our second lengthy interview, she had spent over 3 hours at the hospital, and was interviewed by CPS yesterday. She is living in a temporary foster home facing an unknown future. It was too much for anyone. I put down my pen, writing pad and the photos. "Maybe now is a good time to take a break. I need another cookie. How 'bout you?"

"Yes, please," she said jumping up from the couch. "I need to go potty first," and off she ran.

CHAPTER 25

Shantay and I had an amazing rapport. The momentum had been productive but very taxing on her. It is amazing how stepping away for a few minutes can be so restorative. What we needed was fresh air and a walk. But there wasn't time. As I glanced over the spreadsheet, she returned to the couch and leaned against Leo the Lion. I narrowed the list, aware that more was needed. I could not afford for any decision makers to doubt or discount the evidence. I knew sharing these stories was triggering the emotions and sensations of the original injury. But having the details was vital, in fact, I was more convinced than ever that her life depended on me bringing irrefutable evidence to the commonwealth attorney.

Ms. Tyler had no information about the scar on Shantay's chin. She was only certain it happened during this school year. I withdrew photo #9 but instead of showing her, I placed my finger on my chin. "Do you remember what happened here?"

"Yes, that was last Christmas. Everyone was excited, but I was missing Anita. I woke up feeling alone, more alone than I ever felt before. Christmas was not the same without her and I wished she were there. When I heard the boys were awake, I went upstairs. Momma had baked three huge pans of breakfast casserole. The boys were gobbling down their food as fast as momma could fill someone's plate. I waited till they were done. Everyone was happy and even momma was laughing and smiling. When I told her good morning, Momma, Merry Christmas, she even said Merry Christmas back, and told me to get my plastic plate. When I held it up, she scraped a big spoonful from the last pan. She even added a piece of toast with jelly that was left on somebody's plate. I never eat the food she feeds the family, so I was excited. It smelled delicious.

"The living room is not big enough for me, so I was sitting on the floor near the dining room. They were all together in a circle. When I leaned against the wall, I was hidden behind the couch like I was not even there. I wanted to be with the family, but they were happier when I was not around. They never talked about Anita, and I missed her so much.

The boys were laughing and talking and taking turns passing out presents. They were stacked up higher than the couch. I had three. I took small bites of my food and watched the colorful lights blinking on the Christmas Tree. I thought it was the prettiest thing I had ever seen.

"I did not want to hurry through opening my presents like the boys were. I picked up my green plastic plate and ate more egg casserole. My food was cold but much better than cereal with water. When I finally opened my first present, it was a pack of underwear. It had the days of the week on the waistband. Momma gives me new ones every year. I had two more presents to open. I leaned forward and stretched my neck to see past the couch. The boys had toys and games and clothes everywhere. I leaned back against the wall and thought about Anita. I wondered if she knew it was Christmas. Did she miss me too?

"Anita and I always sat together when we opened presents on Christmas morning. Even though the family left us out sometimes, we had each other. As long as I can remember, it was me and her. Now, it's just me. But mamma gave me a real breakfast and I tried to think about the good things. I leaned against the wall so no one could see me. My ears and face got warm, and I wanted to cry. I blinked and bit my lip, but I could not stop the tears. I did not make a sound, and I kept wiping my tears away hoping they would stop. I knew Momma would get mad if she saw me crying. She would say I was spoiling Christmas with a bad attitude, and I was ungrateful for breakfast and presents. If momma let me eat breakfast, she might let me eat Christmas dinner too unless she gets mad.

"I kept wiping my nose on my sleeve, but I needed a tissue. I thought if I could sneak away, they might not notice. But when I stood up, I stepped on my plate, and it flipped over. My breakfast casserole and toast went on the carpet. I could not let momma see. I tried to scoop it back onto the plate before she saw. When I looked up, she was standing over me."

" I knew you were up to something."

"Before I could explain she hit my back and shoulder from behind."

"You spilled food on my carpet, didn't you. I knew I should not give you something nice. And you wonder why I don't. Now, take your butt downstairs and I do not want to see your face or hear a peep out of you."

"Please can I stay upstairs? I promise I will be good. I don't want to miss out on Christmas.' She did not even answer me. She just lifted the stick over her head, and I knew she was going to swing it again harder. I tried to get up and run, but when I turned around to go downstairs, she hit my chin with the board. I mess up everything. I ruined Christmas. Momma is right, I am stupid and clumsy."

"Anita was the only one I had and I was missing her so much. After Anita fell and hurt her head she was in a wheelchair. She could not talk anymore, and I couldn't tell if she understood anything. Sometimes I would talk to her, and she would stare away. But sometimes she would look at me like she wanted to say something. The day she got sick at school and the ambulance took her to the hospital, I never saw her again. I never got to say goodbye. She was my best friend and the only person that loved me. I spent a few weeks with another family, but I was away from Anita. I talked with a nice lady and a police officer, but I do not remember his name. They asked me lots of questions like you Detective Meadows. Momma was meaner to Anita before. Back then she hit me with a baseball bat, and I got stitches a few times, but not every day like now.

"I was scared when they took me back home and Anita was gone. I cried every night when I was alone. Nobody told me what happened, and I did not understand why Momma said she was never coming back. She said Anita was living in a home with other kids in wheelchairs and I would never see her again. She told me not to talk about her or mention her name again. She even said Anita did not miss me or know who I am. I tried so hard not to think about Anita. I never want to forget her or stop talking about her.

"Anita is only a year older than me, but she is so smart. Well, I guess that was before she got hurt. She read better than me and when she had to read for school, she let me sit beside her and listen. She was pretty and had lots of friends at school. Kids don't want to be friends with me because one of my eyes looks funny. I always wanted to be like her. When she finished her chores, we spent time together. She was my only friend. We shared secrets and sometimes we talked about how mean mom was and how stupid the boys are. When momma would beat her, she hardly ever cried. She was stronger than me. She told me after momma whipped me or smacked my head with the stick that I should try not to cry. If I had a bad day at school, or the boys were mean, Anita would hug me and tell me, 'Everything is going to be all right. We have each other and that is all we need.' When the boys would watch wrestling or basketball on TV, we would play cards or checkers. Sometimes after momma whipped her, she would tell me, 'When we get older, we are going to leave here, and I will take care of you. I will protect you and keep you safe.' Now I am all alone. She will never live with me, and no one will take me away and protect me. There is no one to read with me or hug me when I am sad. I don't know if I will ever see her again. She moved far away, and momma said she will never take me to visit her. Detective Meadows, I don't know what to do without her. I was sad before, but we had each other."

Shantay stopped talking and she dropped her head. Her sorrow could not be contained, and big tears cascaded. She did not try to repress them but tried to cover her face. She did not utter a sound, but the grief was deafening. I wondered how long it had been since she had cried in someone's presence.

The fierce bond of sisterhood was the only certainty she had known. It had been ripped from her cruelly and without explanation. There was no one to reach for or turn to. No source of comfort or affection. Shantay's sudden and unexplained separation from her sister had been deeply impactful. Anita's absence had exacerbated Shantay's fears and magnified the isolation and loneliness. Shantay had been denied answers and forced to suppress her emotions. Her caregivers not only abandoned her to suffer in silence and isolation, but compounded her pain by escalating their abuse. As a father of two children, I wanted to scoop her up in my arms and take her pain away.

I pulled a tissue from the box, handed it to her and set the box close by. She blew her nose and reached for another tissue. I felt powerless. Nothing I could say or do would change what had happened to her. Nothing can restore what was stolen or unfairly denied. Shantay would wrestle with unanswered questions all her life. Most of us do; but very few from such an early age. There were no words that could ease her pain and I dared not interrupt or force words into silence.

Years of interviewing hundreds of child victims taught me to be patient in these unbearable moments. To push past it is to deny or diminish the gravity of her loss. Grief is a sacred language that is communicated without words. I tried to imagine one of my children losing their sibling, enduring the loss while forbidden to express sorrow or mention their absence. It was inconceivable.

~

It broke my heart to realize, at ten years old, Shantay had never experienced a real Christmas or even known the joy of the Christmas spirit. My parents dedicated themselves to making it special for me and my brother. During Christmas break, we bought, wrapped, gave, and opened presents while visiting family. We feasted and ate special desserts, baked goodies, and confections. My favorite was mom's potato candy! She made dough from potatoes and sugar and then spread peanut butter on it and rolled it up. It was an extra special treat we looked forward to every year, and reserving it for Christmastime made it even more special.

My childhood Christmases resembled the cover of a JC Penny catalog. In the weeks leading up to Christmas, Dad would take on side work, such as upholstering furniture, to ensure they could afford presents.

Selecting the Christmas tree was a much-anticipated family outing. Mom would fill a thermos with hot coffee for her and dad and another one with cocoa for us. We would head into the woods and search for the perfect tree. One of my first Christmas memories was having a tree so big and round that it filled a huge space in our small living room. Our parents went all out to make Christmas special. On Christmas morning the tree would be surrounded by presents. Santa always brought toys to entertain us. As we grew and our interests evolved, Santa's goal remained the same, to entertain two curious and rambunctious boys.

In a Christmas photo taken when we were young, my brother is a toddler sitting on the floor in front of the couch. It was early, we were dressed in matching pajamas, still sleepy eyed but grinning with delight. I remember the magic of knowing Santa had visited our house during the night. I was five years old, and on the couch above my brother. I have a board game in my lap, and beside by brother is a line of toy trucks from Santa. The dump truck, a battery-operated semi-truck with a crane on the trailer, a bulldozer, and a red and white plastic go-cart. Perfect toys for little boys, plenty to share and the promise of hours of fun.

Another memory of Christmas was when I was eight. My parents gave me a cassette tape recorder. I taped our conversations Christmas morning and then when we opened gifts at grandpa's house. I still have that tape and can hear myself grumbling about having to bring in coal for the fire.

Such wonderful memories are deeply woven into the fabric of our family. I cannot imagine a childhood without a single moment of parental affection and wonder.

~

"Detective Meadows?"

"Yes, Shantay, I am listening. I'm sorry. I got distracted for a moment writing my notes. You were telling me about what happened last Christmas after I asked about the scar on your chin. Please, finish sharing what happened." She was silent.

"Shantay, can you look at me? You are not stupid, and you did nothing wrong. Everyone drops and spills things. You are a smart girl and braver than any ten-year-old I have ever met. Do you want to know what I think? I think Anita would be proud of how strong you are sharing these terrible stories with me. I am glad we met. I will always remember that we shared warm chocolate chip cookies and a glass of milk. Do you understand me?" She did not speak or look up.

CHAPTER 26

"I know you are tired sweetie. I need to ask you one more question. We are almost done, I promise. Can you tell me what happened here," I asked holding up picture #1. The photo zoomed in on a thick scar that zig-zagged from her upper lip to the bottom of her nostril. It had been a deep gash. The scar was wide and indented, as if not pulled together by stitches or staples. Ms. Tyler thought it had been stitched after Mrs. Hunter was contacted by the school, but it must have been several days after the injury.

"That happened near the beginning of school. I remember because three of my brothers have birthdays kinda close together. Momma gave them a big cookout for their birthday. She didn't work that day and when I got home from school everything was picked up, so momma told me to clean the bathroom again.

"She bought the boys a giant chocolate cake with chocolate frosting and Happy Birthday with frosting. The boys got to have friends over and the older boys were playing football in the back yard. I got to stay outside but momma said to keep my mouth shut and stay out of the way. Daddy cooked hotdogs on the grill and even gave me one with some chips. Momma gave him a funny look and told me, 'Don't you think you're getting any birthday cake.'

"When all the kids went home, momma handed me a big trash bag and told me to pick up all the trash and put all the toys where they belonged before I come inside.

"I cleaned off the picnic tables, then walked all around dragging the big trash bag. I knew if momma found any paper plates, cups, and napkins when she checked I would get a whipping, so I walked all around. When I found a plate with some cake left on it, I didn't throw it away. I put the cake in a napkin and hid it in the shed. It was almost dark, but I got the trash picked up and all the toys put away. I snuck up the back steps and looked in the glass door. They were sitting in the living room watching TV, but no one saw me. I know I should have thrown that cake away, but I wanted to taste it. So, I snuck back to the shed and ate it. I felt bad because momma told me I couldn't have any, but it was delicious.

"When I knocked on the door, momma came out and asked if I was ready for her to inspect the yard. 'Yes ma'am. I picked up all the toys and all the trash."

"What in the world are you so happy about?" she asked.

"Nothing, except daddy gave me a hotdog and chips, that's all. And I'm happy I got to be outside with everybody for the birthday cookout."

"When I smiled, she got a really mean look and she grabbed my arm. 'What do I see in your teeth? Is that chocolate? Did you sneak a piece of cake?'

"No ma'am. I just found some left on a plate and I tasted some after I finished my work.' She kept squeezing my arm harder and yelled at daddy to bring her the stick. I tried to pull away and that made her madder. Then she hit my head so hard, I fell and busted my lip too. I woke up later, when it was dark. The lights were on inside, I had a bad headache, and I was sick to my stomach. I didn't know what to do. One of the older boys walked into the kitchen and saw me. He opened the door and threw a big rag at me and put ice in a baggie and told me to put it on my forehead. Then he shut the door, turned the lock, and pulled the blinds. I felt dizzy and laid down. When I woke up again, it was nighttime. No lights were on inside the house, but I could see they put the plastic bucket outside.

"Detective Meadows, I don't want to talk anymore."

During the home search we did not walk out the kitchen door, onto the back deck or down the back steps. If we had, I may have noticed a blood stain. I could picture the scene unfolding on their bi-level deck. I could see her lying in the dark, the family content to leave her there. How many ways could I apologize for what has been done to her? I wondered if she would ever enjoy a piece of birthday cake without being reminded of that day.

How do I bring our time together to an end? How do I walk away after stirring up these hellish memories again? I hated this part. She could not understand it yet, but her life would never be the same. I was certain she would never be returned to the Hunters. Her rescue was in motion. Shantay had not acted out of spite or disobedience. She had not fabricated a history built on false accusations simply to garner attention. Her scars testified to the truth.

A desire to pray rose from a long forgotten childlike faith. I grew up with a simple faith taught by a country pastor. I never challenged what I learned or pursued religion as an adult. The faith I was taught as a child was cut and dry: if you prayed for traveling mercies, and you arrived safely, God had protected you. If you prayed and there was an accident and someone got hurt, it was not that God had not protected you, but it was not God's fault either. We were taught that when terrible things happen it was God's will. If we suffered, God allowed it.

Sounds a bit unreliable. Why pray if fate is decided? How do you teach such things to a child whose entire life is marked by violence? As an adult I never felt compelled to search for different answers. My life experience did not fit the indifference of that premise. My brother is one of my favorite people in the world. He is a great guy and would do anything for anyone. Yet he suffered tragedy that made no sense at all. Nothing good ever came of it. I watched him live with a broken heart, not once but twice. Personally, I had stowed away religion and compartmentalized what I could not reconcile between life and God.

Something about Shantay's resilience caused an unfamiliar faith to stir. An image of her flashed before me. She was a young woman, no longer defined by her scars, emotionally strong and happy. I wanted to believe it was possible. I was not sure how, but I did not fight for these children to simply resign them to a life of impossibilities because of victimhood. I wrestled with the injustice, but no answers came. I found no theodicy that adequately explained the contradiction of an omniscient and loving God who allowed such evil upon children. Perhaps the God I do not know well can do the impossible for innocents like Shantay who did nothing to deserve the pain they have endured.

I wanted to fight for her chance to rise like a Phoenix from the ashes. I told myself Shantay has time to turn her academics around. She is young enough to reestablish trust. Fear would subside and memories fade and be replaced by better ones. A good counselor could help her work through the pain. For now, her life was in flux and would be for a while. But this horrific chapter was over. There would be no going back. I honestly believed I would witness a miraculous metamorphosis. And I would be on the sidelines cheering her on.

Healthy boundaries between detectives and victims are crucial. If I absorbed the emotional wreckage of each victim's life, I would suffocate. It would hinder my objectivity. There were times balancing my duties and emotion felt more like maneuvering a gyroscope; it would not take much for me to crash. There were occasions when those lines got blurred. I met children like Shantay, and their stories buckled my knees. Compassion overshadowed rules about proper detachment.

CHAPTER 27

I was up early, warm cup of tea in hand. The house was quiet, and I needed some time to strategize and mentally prepare for Monday so we could pull out in a couple of hours and I could enjoy the trip. Planning time away with my family at this point in our lives was always a gamble. My case load was a constant revolving process that necessitated my ability to adapt at a moment's notice. While many cases were suspended in limbo waiting for court dates, new cases were added continually. I never reached a place where everything could be "checked off" this list. I guess some detectives think little of passing on cases, I would never have done so by choice, ever. It was not that I believed myself a better detective; but taking ownership of my responsibilities was, and continues to be, an integral part of my work ethic. It was impossible to predict what I might be in the middle of when it was time to head out of town. There were occasions when I canceled plans, but did I not make it a habit.

Both kids had a full schedule of activities, and even if it was okay to miss band practice, as a group of musicians we committed to being around for shows booked in advance. My family was in a season when spontaneous getaways were rare.

I met Shantay just a few days ago and already made considerable progress in her case. I had hoped to interrogate the Hunters and arrest them for additional charges before my day off. But plans were halted when I was brought a new case and my priorities shifted. Shantay was safe and there was no chance she would be returned to her parents, so I diverted the next steps to Monday, and opened another investigation.

Last night was given to packing the fifth wheel and having as much done in advance as possible. With a few details remaining, we were scheduled to leave promptly at 10:00 am. We planned to arrive late afternoon for an early dinner, stopping for a leisurely picnic lunch along the way. So, I set the alarm, made a cup of hot tea, and sat down at my desk to tie up loose ends. Pressure and stress are relative. I manage both well, to a point. Being prepared is not an option. Mr. Hunter seems a bit of a passive fellow. I would not be surprised if he spoke willingly. Mrs. Hunter, on the other hand, would likely be more reticent this time. I had an idea formulating and I needed to work the process out in my mind so I would not be distracted this weekend. The photos of Shantay would be instrumental in the way I would confront her.

As I lost myself in examining the photos and concentrating on the most effective way to approach the interrogations, a considerable amount of time passed. I heard Becky in the kitchen and realized two hours had passed. I am a stickler for leaving on time and arriving on time. We had a scheduled time to depart, and I had a few tasks to complete before then. I was grateful I opted not to go into the office this morning.

We never had to coerce the kids to go camping. These adventures were woven into the heritage we wanted to impart. Passing the baton of an enriched childhood to the next generation was important to us. Even at an age when their peers were primarily focused on being with friends, our kids still enjoyed being with their parents and each other. Of course, the Baker's had children close in age to Holly and Mark and they had grown up sharing these adventures. I like to think that was icing on the cake. I knew in the years to come their independence would pull them further away. For now, I could not think of anything more meaningful.

Becky strolled into my office her hands cupped around a mug of warm tea. I looked up from my paperwork, "Good morning, Beck. I am wrapping things up. I have a really big case I am working on, and it has been a tough week. I am glad we are getting away, but there is a lot going on at the office. I was called into another case last Wednesday; the grand jury meets in four days, and I have evidence to present for a case that has been waiting to be heard for months. I just need to get my head straight so I can enjoy the weekend. Are the kids up yet? I want to pull out of the driveway at 10:00."

"Mark is, I made sure he got up before I came down. He is in the shower. Holly spent the night with a friend, remember? She will be home at 9:00."

I glanced at the clock; it was 8:15. "I wish she hadn't spent the night elsewhere. We have a plan, and I expect to leave on time. John and Mary are timing dinner to be ready upon our arrival, and I will not keep them waiting. Every time Holly stays with the Patterson's they bring her home willy-nilly. Has Mrs. Patterson ever been on time?"

"Rick please do not spoil your morning worrying about something that might not happen. Come on, I will make some breakfast. Would you like me to heat up the kettle for more tea?"

~

At 9:45 a.m., all the prepared food was packed in the coolers and the coolers stowed in the truck. We were ready to go, and Holly was not home. My eyes were burning a hole in my watch as I watched the seconds tick by. Clearly it was not helping matters but I consider keeping others waiting blatantly disrespectful. To me it says your time is not valuable, so I am never late. It may be my biggest pet peeve and definitely the easiest way to set me off when I am stressed. My wife and kids know this about me. Pretty much anyone that knows me, knows that. As much as I did not want to be cross, but impatience got the best of me. "She better not expect us to wait while she takes a shower when she comes rolling in." Becky did not respond to my remark.

Becky and Mark were in the truck, and I was standing outside the driver's door scanning the road. At precisely 10:00 a.m. Mrs. Patterson's Honda Accord pulled in the driveway. She lowered her window. "Good morning, y'all. See, Holly is home right on time for y'all to have a fun weekend," she said waving a bit cheerier than I thought necessary. Her version of being "on time" is different than mine. Holly walked towards us with her pillow folded in her arms, and her backpack over her shoulder. She opened the door and tossed them in the seat and asked, "Is the door still unlocked? I need to use the bathroom before we leave."

Before I could say something I would regret, Becky got out of the truck, unlocked the door and asked Holly to hurry. It was 10:15 before we pulled out of the driveway and stopped speaking, nursing my irritation. In fact, the truck remained silent for well over an hour before anyone said a word. We pulled into a rest stop so Becky could stretch her legs, and probably to interrupt the needle stuck in the groove of my own gloomy thoughts. Once back on the highway, my mood had shifted somewhat. The interruption helped.

I glanced in the rearview mirror and watched my kids. Holly was reading a magazine and Mark was playing an electronic game. It is strange watching your children become young men and women before your eyes, and I felt the sting of time slipping away.

Mark is rugged but personable. He is the guy everyone wants to be around. I credit Becky for his endearing charm and approachability. He has an infectious calm that will be a powerful influence on others someday. He is naturally positive, levelheaded, a contemplator, but creative. He loves working with his hands and is always willing to learn something new.

Holly is more like me. She is audacious and willing to plow through barriers and redefine boundaries if she believes the cause is worth it. She is a natural leader, willing to take a stand and fight for what she believes in. Her passion can move mountains. But she easily transitions from focused and responsible to vivacious and witty. The party starts when Holly walks in the room. Her laughter is as big as her life. She is tenacious and fiercely loyal.

In the seasons of working night shifts I was always mindful of how I felt when my dad was gone. I never wanted to be an absent parent, even for a brief time, but it came with the job. Through it all we raised two amazing human beings who knew they were loved and had not gone off the rails into rebellion or drugs. I felt truly blessed and annoyed with myself for being so impatient. Darn it, she knows I hate to be late.

Becky finally broke the silence. "I would like to plant Sunflowers this year. That newly cleared patch of land is flooded with sunlight. I bet they would thrive back there. I read they are easy growers. If we plant a new row every 2 weeks, they will bloom continuously until the first frost. Wouldn't that be great for family photos?"

"I love that idea. Sounds fun," I responded hoping to leave the morning behind.

CHAPTER 28

We rolled up to the camp site while John was still grilling the burgers. The aroma of Angus beef over an open flame filled the air. As soon as the truck was in park, the kids jumped out and ran to their friends. Mary Baker walked over and wrapped her arms around Becky. Our families took turns arriving the first afternoon and preparing an early dinner. John waved from the fire pit, and I moseyed over. Baked beans were bubbling in a cast iron pot and Becky brought everyone's favorite homemade potato salad.

There was a huge picnic table draped in a bright red and white checkered tablecloth. Strands of twinkle lights were draped between three large trees and the Bakers' camper. Strategically placed tiki lights stood guard like soldiers keeping the insects at bay. Their flames swayed gently with the breeze. Such a welcoming ambiance.

A large stack of dry firewood and a heaping box of kindling was next to the fire pit. Several camp chairs were around it. Two guitar stands were positioned close by, one cradling John's acoustic guitar. The other was waiting for mine. The moon will be full this weekend. There was no chance of rain and the temperatures were idyllic. By nightfall, a million stars would become our canopy. These are the moments we live for.

We had camped with the Bakers for years. Everyone got along beautifully. John and I shared a love for family, camping and music. Mary and Becky had bonded over having children, gardening and husbands who loved their families, camping and music. Our children are similar in age and grew up like cousins. "We are so glad to see everyone," Mary said pulling Becky and I together for a bear hug. "We have missed you guys."

"We missed you too," Becky replied. "Thanks for setting up camp. Everything looks magical, like a photo for 'how to create the perfect camp site.' It feels like coming home. There is no place we would rather be. The kids have been studying for exams and we are almost at the finish line for the school year. Spring sports and cheering had us running in circles." She glanced at me with softness in her eyes. "Rick's been busy at work, even his commitment to leave by 5 o'clock has been challenging. He does not say much about it, but the responsibility is taxing. The timing of this weekend was perfect, it is just what we all needed." Her words rose like a gentle prayer, followed by a collective silence.

We ate our fill and then some. John helped me set up the fifth wheel, at least what could not wait until morning. The ladies stowed the food and washed the dishes. John stoked the fire and added more wood as everyone gathered around. The flames increased and seemed to reach heavenward. John and I strummed our favorite melodies, and everyone sang along. I was mesmerized by the dancing flames. The rising moon was beaming through the trees illuminating the night. It captured a moment when all felt right in the world.

Lulled by the crackling fire, I closed my eyes to relish in the well-being filling me. The forest felt like a sanctuary; and the love of my family and friends created a fortress shielding me from the cares of the world. Beneath the vast moonlit sky, our voices rose in harmony and penetrated the darkness like an anthem.

Raptured in perfect peace, a haunting voice, just above a whisper pierced the calm. It was Shantay pleading, "Please don't make me go back home."

The sound of her voice was so vivid I opened my eyes and looked around. My fingers moved instinctively across the strings keeping perfect time with the song long ago memorized. I had stopped singing though and turned my attention to the small voice that interrupted my bliss.

The voice was not audible, but as clear as if someone were speaking: "She has never known a moment like this, filled with peace and wonder surrounded by people she loves. She has no one to rely on, no one protecting her. She has never experienced the comfort and shelter, of the unconditional love of an adult. I have brought you to her to help rescue her. I have seen her pain; I have heard her cries in the night. You are my answer."

Faith was not a primary focus in my life; but it had been a quiet and steady undercurrent since childhood. There were times in my law enforcement career when I reached an impasse working on a case and I would receive insight or wisdom unexpectedly. Those moments felt surreal. An idea would interrupt and direct me to something I had not considered. I would review a witness's statement or be drawn to a piece of evidence. I would "see" and know what to do. Following those prompts helped me solve several cases and brought positive outcomes. A coworker would suggest it sounded like divine intervention which piqued my curiosity. As intriguing as it sounded, the notion that the God I sang about in Sunday school led police officers to solve crimes seemed far-fetched.

Then I joined the Crimes Against Children Taskforce and every belief I loosely held unraveled. One of my first cases involved a 6-month-old baby. Graphic details are not necessary for anyone to imagine the unspeakable harm caused by a grown man repeatedly raping an infant. It became increasingly more challenging to believe in God. The stream of unanswered "why's" slowly eroded the foundation of my youth. Where was God when such unspeakable harm is forced upon an infant, a toddler, or any child? I could not reconcile the contradiction and began questioning if God were real. If I accept that God was real, how can he be good and allow such things? Try explaining that to the parent of an infant requiring reconstructive surgery. I could not reason through the reality I was exposed to when it collided with the God of my vacation Bible school. No one could explain it and their lame attempts seemed insulting. At times, the evil I compartmentalized brought the loneliest isolation in the world.

When I was not feeling guilty or outraged, my defenses would soften. After winning a few cases and seeing justice served, my guard would drop. Something would remind me of the compassion my grandpa exuded. That God had faded some, or I had silenced his voice. That God wanted children rescued. That God despised the pain and suffering they endured. For the first time in years, I thought perhaps God had invaded this moment and had something to say. I listened intently to the silence for what felt like an eternity. I turned my thoughts to focus entirely on Shantay. I never heard another sound. I felt vulnerable, desperate to protect this young girl. If the God of my childhood was not the truest version, then a God I did not know well wanted me to help him rescue children. I needed his help to do that. A simple prayer rose from the depths of my heart, "Lord, please help me. Please help me rescue her."

~

I awakened the next day before dawn. Becky stirred as I pulled the cover over her. I stoked the smoldering embers and added several pieces of firewood. The early morning songbirds kept me company. Breakfast would be a feast of fresh ground sausage patties flavored with cumin, sage, garlic, and a hit of red pepper. I reserved a hearty part of the sausage to brown and crumble for my famous savory sausage gravy. All will be served over browned-to-perfection biscuits with their choice of made-to-order farm fresh eggs. I enjoyed a few moments of quiet, noting the crystal-clear skies we enjoyed last night were grey and overcast.

When I felt a few drops of moisture hit me, I didn't think much of it. Clouds do not necessarily mean rain. The forecast had not called for rain. Perhaps they were merely dewdrops falling from the trees. A few turned to several and without further warning the clouds burst open and steady rain was falling. I covered the gravy, moved the biscuits off direct heat and dashed to the camper.

You have got to be kidding me. Pouring rain. How could the forecast change that much? I grabbed my rain jacket and headed back to the fire, now fizzling and smoking. My open flame feast was spoiled by mother nature's version of how the day would go. Massive clouds had rolled in, shrouding any possibility of sunshine. I felt annoyance rising and stretching my patience like a rubber band.

Before I could shout John's name, he was beside me with a giant golf umbrella open above me and my assembly of cast iron cookware. Becky and Mary pulled chairs and whatever they could grab under the awnings that extended from our campers. I pulled the skillets off the now saturated embers and tried to laugh it off. No one expects a camping trip to be perfect, how unrealistic is that? The key is playing for contingencies. We always brought cards and a propane hotplate just in case. Mary filled the enamel kettle with water and clicked on the hotplate while Becky put teabags in our cups as we waited for the water to boil.

The kids, still sound asleep, were oblivious. The adults huddled together beneath the canvas canopy trying to make the best of an unexpected, and increasingly more disappointing, morning. Until the winds blew the rain sidewise.. Gone were any chances to hike, fish or salvaging the fire pit. Everything was a muddy mess and temps were chilly, not to mention damp and windy. The prospect of playing cards for hours would typically have sufficed. Not today. Without mentioning it to Becky first, the thought I had been ruminating on, slipped out. "I'm sorry guys. I can't do this today. We're going to pack it up and head home."

CHAPTER 29

When I returned to work on Monday morning I was not as rested or as mentally prepared as I hoped to be. My thoughts returned to the Friday evening campfire when, for a moment, the world seemed right and good. I felt bad for spoiling things. But I knew how to be professional. This time, I tucked away a less than stellar weekend and thoughts of the family I loved but disappointed. I sequestered myself in my office to concentrate.

In less than a week I had obtained a wealth of evidence. It was time to abridge the data and integrate the pertinent facts into my incident report.

Incident reports often began as a brief document. As the investigation ensues supplements are added, and it can become quite lengthy. The synopsis of my second interview with Shantay focused on details that augment her previous statement and incorporate further details about specific scars.

Constructing a comprehensive police report from a plethora of facts is a skill I developed through trial and error. The learning curve included knowing what to omit that could be challenged later by lawyers. Investigations are not cut and dry. Having the "smoking gun" is an exception. You learn not to embarrass yourself or the department by presenting half-ass cases that cannot withstand the litmus test. The prosecutor will scrutinize your findings. Their reputation and, by extension, the County's reputation are at stake. If you have reasonable doubt, you can expect that others will. Inept police work does not result in convictions.

Stick with the facts. No one cares what I feel, or believe, or suspect. What solid evidence do I have and how can I explicitly connect that evidence to the accused? If I were on the other side, would I be convinced? If the Commonwealth Attorney's office is the gatekeeper to the courtroom, you better bring an army of facts. If they were behind you, they gave it all they had. If they felt the defense attorney had wiggle room, they spared the court the wasted time. If there was a risk of it being thrown out, it never made it past their desk.

It was my responsibility to take all the threads and weave them together and draft my report. The compilation of data would be built around a timeline and link to every piece of evidence we had. No one could review the facts and believe anything less than persistent and worsening physical, psychological, and emotional abuse.

Although it felt like a contradiction, the strategy will be to eventually request the first charges be "Nolle Prosequi" (when the prosecution agrees to take no further action). This is different from dismissing the charges. I will arrest them again once I decide the full extent of charges. I would leave nothing to chance or luck. In less than a week I had obtained a wealth of evidence. I turned my attention to amalgamating facts.

I spoke with Jami who briefed me on the interview at CPS with the Hunters. She confirmed that they planted the "seed" that PD discovered blood on the end of the 3-foot piece of lumber. Mrs. Hunter responded instantly with a fabricated story. She claimed that Mr. Hunter noticed Shantay repeatedly hitting herself in the face with a stick. After that Mr. Hunter watched her sneak into the living room and hide it under the couch thinking no one had seen her.

When Jami asked Mrs. Hunter about the injury to Shantay's arm, she reiterated that Shantay had fallen through the springs on the trampoline. Mrs. Hunter backtracked from this story with school personnel when the facts did not concur with the timeline. When I spoke with Mrs. Hunter, she claimed Shantay must have slammed her arm against the bathroom vanity to self-injure before school.

Mrs. Hunter described Shantay's lip injury as occurring when the dog knocked her down. In her opinion the cut was not serious, but she reported taking her for medical intervention immediately. This contradicts school records indicating Shantay came to school with her lip ripped open and skin hanging. School personnel had to insist that Mrs. Hunter take her to be seen by a doctor. She emphatically stated that Shantay sleeps in the upper bunk in the upstairs bedroom and three of her sons sleep in the other bunk beds in that room. Mrs. Hunter's sons contradicted this, confirming the child sleeps on the concrete floor in the utility room. Mrs. Hunter unapologetically disclosed that Shantay is not permitted to use dishes other family members use. She claimed this was recommended by a doctor to protect the spread of Shantay's herpes.

~

I obtained ten warrants for Mrs. Hunter: seven counts of malicious wounding, one for administering a caustic substance, one for replacing a medication with a poison, and a malicious wounding for her sister Anita's case three years earlier. I also obtained two warrants for Mr. Hunter: one for burning her with the light bulb. and the other for replacing the medication with poison.

Both subjects were arrested and brought to headquarters.

Interrogation rooms are designed for discomfort. Suspects are sequestered in spaces insulated from distraction and noise. The smell of disinfectant and minimal furniture elicit an institutional feel. Blank concrete brick walls enforce the sense of confinement and impenetrability. Detainees are brought into the vexing space containing nothing more than a metal table and two metal chairs. A suspect is often left alone to heighten the pressure. Florescent bulbs omit muted light while spotlights draw attention to the table. A two-way mirror fills a third of the wall, reflecting light and casting shadowy silhouettes. A suspect might remain handcuffed and, when particularly agitated or under the influence, an additional officer will stand guard.

Mrs. Hunter was escorted into the condemning space. The clunk of the steel bolt locking behind her was an apropos symbol of her fate. I studied her through the two-way mirror. She paced for a few minutes and surveyed the space, avoiding her reflection. She finally sat down, her rotund body drooping over the edges of the steel chair. She shifted her weight several times, leaning forward on the table. Several minutes passed before I entered.

Since our initial meeting three days prior, I had obtained copious amounts of evidence. As facts were gathered, I compiled and evaluated them, consolidating everything into a compendium of facts. We were not reliant on DNA evidence to support the charges.

Every shred of evidence strengthened my initial assessment; that Mrs. Hunter is a tyrannical and deranged monster who used the pretext of adoption to draw two innocent girls into her dungeon of duplicity. From the onset she exploited and demoralized vulnerable children to feed an insatiable bloodthirst.

When Mrs. Hunter was summoned to the school and led to believe she was consenting for Shantay to be taken to the hospital, it reinforced the illusion that her deeds remained undiscovered. In fact, she had no say in the matter. During the first interview her responses were curt and antagonist. Her contempt for Shantay was shameless. Arrogance and disregard for the law blinded her from comprehending the unfolding events. She armored up, resolutely denying any wrongdoing or ill treatment toward the child. Her reality was so distorted she never hid her emotional detachment and readily acknowledged her parental authority was justified. She crafted a narrative, which shifted blame, vindicated herself, and vilified both girls. Her actions, that of a sociopath, exhibited no conscience, believed she was above the law, and/or deluded herself into believing her behaviors were permissible. Up to now, no one held her accountable, making her overconfident and galvanizing her delusion.

Reports, prior contact with CPS, corroborating statements, and photographs had fortified the case. We had ironclad evidence capable of steamrolling through her bastion of lies and vanishing them into thin air. She had no defense.

When I stepped into the interrogation room, the deputy closed the door with a thud that echoed off the block walls. Then the steel bolt locked with an ominous clunk. I sat across from Mrs. Hunter. "And so, we meet again," I began.

After reading Mrs. Hunter her Miranda rights, she folded her arms and looked me square in the eyes and said, "I want an attorney, and I ain't saying another word."

"No problem, Mrs. Hunter. But I have a few things to say to you. We will not leave this room until I have said them. And when I am done, you will be taken out in handcuffs. You will stand before the magistrate. You will be processed for detainment, and you will spend the night in jail. In the meantime, I am going to show you exactly what I have based my charges on."

And I began to unload.

"When I met with you previously, it was after spending an hour and a half with Shantay. And I know you have managed to frighten the child into keeping your hateful secrets for many years now. But Shantay was not afraid to talk to me. In fact, she told me much more than yes or no answers. And unlike the others you have deluded, I believe her. I believe every word she told me is the truth, just like where she said we would find the items you use to beat, whip, and poison her. And Shantay trusted the child trauma specialist that examined more than just her arm. During her three-hour visit at the hospital, we learned a great deal. While she was being examined a police forensic tech obtained forty photographs.

"I have those photographs in my possession, all substantiating what Shantay reported experiencing at your hand. And the other day, I spent another hour and a half with Shantay, and we talked about these wounds and scars, blisters, burns and lacerations. I want to make myself perfectly clear, Mrs. Hunter. We believe her. Shantay was fearless about sharing exactly what you did to her behind closed doors. I know what life was like for her at home. She did not hold back.

"As you know, we confiscated the 3-foot piece of lumber that has tape on one end and blood on the other. We have the metal cable with a curly wire, which had several strands of hair tangled in it. We located the eyedrops bottle with contents that smell like ammonia. All were under the couch where you keep them for easy access. We confiscated the foot shaped rubber mat that she used for sleeping on the concrete floor. And we have the plastic bucket you forced her to urinate and defecate in. Both were found in the backyard. Those items are being processed and sent to the crime lab for forensic analysis. But do not think that buys you time. We have ample evidence that does not require us to wait for DNA results. There is no doubt about your guilt.

"When Shantay was examined by the child trauma specialist, due to the condition of her body, she ordered multiple x-rays, not just her arm. They did blood work and urinalysis. The pediatrician confirmed that not only are the wounds that cover her entire body too numerous to count, but Shantay has been starved. Shantay is suffering from severe malnutrition. She is anemic, and lab results indicate she is suffering from liver damage. Mrs. Hunter, Shantay is the same weight she was three years ago, and she devoured two meals while she was there.

"Despite your insistence that Shantay be 'contained' in a classroom with developmentally delayed children, the doctor indicated Shantay was able to comprehend and respond to questions at an age-appropriate level.

"Despite your claims that the child is unruly, unmanageable, and acts violently to self and others, personnel described her as alert, pleasant, and cooperative.

"Shantay described the same forms of abuse to the pediatrician that she shared with me, including the burning eye drops and continual food deprivation. She also recounted an incident where you forced her legs to bend backwards so far it caused her to walk with a limp.

"I took those photographs with me when I visited Shantay. She and I discussed many of those scars and when and how they happened. Shantay's memory is very clear, and she provided vivid details about the events that led to those injuries. Many of those details are corroborated by dated notes captured by school personnel and attendance records.

"We have reviewed all prior CPS reports, 9-1-1 calls, and records from multiple medical and mental health facilities. Statements include concerns about her and Anita's safety beginning as early as three months after the girls came to live with you. These concerns continued through the year prior to the adoption being formalized, including your ability to parent. I have no doubt that you caused Anita's injuries, and when she was permanently removed, you turned and unleashed your fury upon Shantay. There is no excuse for what you have done.

"Mrs. Hunter, during the formal adoption proceedings, you stood before a judge, an attorney, and the children's guardian ad litem, and after being sworn in, offered testimony as to why you thought it was in the best interest of the girls that their adoption be formally approved. The 'best interests' included considering their 'happiness, security, mental health, and emotional development.' Somehow you convinced the court that you had the capacity to parent two girls in addition to your seven sons. Yet, from the moment I met you, it was clear that you are a bully and a pathological liar. Unlike those you managed to deceive and manipulate, I do not believe a word you've said to me. This illusion of control is over. You are no longer in control of anything.

"Here are the new facts: Shantay will never be returned to you. You will be exposed for the monster you are. You will be held accountable for the things that you have done. You may feel no guilt or shame, but you will feel the consequences.

"You will be fired from your job as a personal care assistant. Your convictions will be registered with the U.S. Department of Health & Human Services, Office of Inspector General and your name added on the List of Excluded Individuals/Entities permanently banishing you from employment in any caregiving capacity. You will go to prison; I hope for an exceedingly long time. If it were up to me, you would never be released. Your felony convictions will follow you for the rest of your life."

I opened the folder of images. I had arranged them in consecutive order, beginning with the crown of her head and ending with the soles of her feet.

"You cannot claim to have not seen the damage you inflicted on her. In fact, I believe you enjoyed ensuring no matter where she looked on her body there would be reminders of your disdain. Not a soul on earth would believe you did not notice. You further humiliate the child by exposing her uncovered flesh to every member of the family as she cleans the bathroom wearing only underwear. Yet you demand she cover her body in long sleeves and layers, even in the scorching heat of summer.

175

"If her scars were counted, it would be hundreds. Not an inch of her flesh is unblemished. These photos confirm a calculated intent to systematically mark her body. You were ensuring she would never escape the reminders of your hatred."

I turned my attention to the first photo. As I began to describe each image with explicit detail, I laid the corresponding photo on the table before her. I brought forty photographs; twenty-two focused on individual scars, the others captured larger areas of her body. It was tough to stomach.

"The first picture was taken after examining her scalp. Readily visible between her braids is a deep gash. Other views show several smaller wounds. These indicate multiple thrashings with the curly wire that ripped skin and pulled hair from the roots.

"Look at that child's face. Look at her eyes swollen almost shut. Her left eye is barely open. What can be seen is how grey and cloudy it is. What kind of human has such a depraved imagination. She has scars on both cheeks. I wonder was that blank fury or were you hoping to blind her.

"The next few images concentrate on significant wounds on her face. I will begin with her forehead, and this close-up of her left eyebrow. Multiple scars. I wonder if you remember the insignificant infraction that resulted in you using brute strength to pummel her with that 3-foot stick. Shantay remembers.

"In this photograph they zoomed in on the flesh torn from the center of her lip to her nostril. This is one of the injuries you attempted to ignore. You sent her to school with it gaping open, her skin flapping down. She could not even close her mouth or talk. This is an injury you did not believe was serious enough to have medically treated. This injury is one of a few that the school had to contact you and insist that you take the child to be seen by a medical professional.

"And this photo of the gash on her chin. Shantay remembers that extra-special Christmas gift you gave her. Not just to ruin that Christmas, but to ensure she never experienced Christmas without thinking of that day. Was it just another twisted way to memorialize how big and powerful you think you are? Did it satisfy your need for violence, or have you become so consumed you can't wait for the next time.

"And the rip on her earlobe. I can picture that morning in the bathroom. As you furiously thrash her face and head, the wire weapon gets caught in her hoop earring. But you did not stop there, you saw a way to cause even more damage. And with inhumane spite, you pulled that curly wire with such tremendous force that her earring ripped through her flesh.

"And this one of her neck and chest. Look at how pronounced her clavicle, shoulders, and sternum are, jutting from her emaciated frame. Was it not enough that she looked like a prisoner from Auschwitz so you decided to whip her across the neck?

"And this work of evil is your husband's; burns from a hot light bulb. that branded her chest. The dad who should be protecting her, standing over her exposed, emaciated body, was outraged because she asked for his help. Instead, she received silence as payback for wanting to complete her forced labor before school. So he sent her a message loud and clear. He backed her into the corner while pressing the metal side of a hot light bulb against her skin. And for extra measure he then rolled it around to leave an oddly distinctive mark. Oh, but that was not enough. These two photos show round two. Grabbing another hot light bulb., this time he pushed the metal tip into the other side of her chest and sustained pressure, singeing her skin. Without mercy, he closed the door and left her in the dark to finish her chore.

"Look at your daughter's ribcage. Mrs. Hunter, you do not get to look away. If you can starve the child, you can look at the damage you inflicted. I want you to comprehend that what I see in this photo is what the trauma specialist saw. And this, all these, will be shown to a judge and jury. Her entire ribcage protrudes, each rib clearly defined, her skin like tissue over her sternum. Her urine and blood samples confirm that Shantay has been starved over an extended period. Years of malnutrition, excessive bleeding and bruising have caused anemia, and the sustained exposure to toxic chemicals caused aplastic anemia. Her calcium level is alarmingly low causing hypocalcemia from long-term vitamin D deficiency. Lab work confirmed multiple indicators that she has sustained liver damage.

"Not only did you deny food at home, you also spitefully denied her food offered freely by the school. The meals your sons ate daily. The child is ten years old, and she weighs 61 pounds. Her weight is the same as it was three years ago. Mrs. Hunter, Shantay ate two meals in the three hours she was at the hospital."

One after the other, I smacked photos on the table creating a collage that would have crumbled a "normal person's" fortified defense. Her eyes and facial expressions never softened.

"Somehow you cannot see what every other civilized human being sees. Look at her hands. Her fingers, swollen thick as sausages, her skin lighter from tips to knuckles, her fingernails yellowed from constant and extended exposure to bleach. I bet you already know how toxic inhaling and absorbing bleach through the skin is. Just another spiteful and premeditated way to poison her.

"Your violence is personal and flagrantly power-based, implying you are punishing the girls to punish someone else. Maybe you resented an irresponsible relative who derailed their life, then expected you to take on their kids. Or maybe it is the sin as old as Cain and Able, unbridled jealousy. Seven times you gave birth, but never had a girl and you resented it. When we met last, you claimed to be a Christian woman. I cannot see where Shantay and Anita fit into that claim. I have never heard of a god that condones brutalizing children. Do you imagine you will escape punishment in this life or the next?

"Look at these photos of her forearm; and this one of both arms side-by-side. Her arm is obviously misshapen, and her wrist was swollen too. Oh, you saw it, you are heartless. In fact, the child you claim is your daughter was taken from you, from your home and not once have you asked how she is. You are not concerned whether she is okay or not.

"This is disgraceful. If you stopped thrashing her long enough to notice the damage, you would see that she looks like a child born into slavery and whipped by a task master. No one could count the lacerations and the scarring where you have sliced through her skin."

Mrs. Hunter's eyes shifted from the table and fixated on the blank wall behind me. Her body tensed and her lips pursed.

"No ma'am, we are not done. And these photos of your adopted daughter's body are precisely why you will be going to jail."

I stared at the next photo in the pile before continuing. I contemplated the wealth of evidence we had obtained. I thought about the sweet girl who spent hours bearing her soul to me. In the photo, Shantay is sitting on the exam table. Her rail thin legs are dangling over the end. The oversized gown has been moved aside to expose the front of her legs. "Mrs. Hunter, if I had only one picture to plead this case, a single photo to convey the entire story of Shantay's life in your home, it would be this one. If I showed this photograph to any judge or jury no words would be necessary." I had strategically placed the expanse of pictures so that even at a glance the totality of her ruthlessness was clear. Then, I placed the final reminder in the very center. Shantay's frail lower legs, so battered and scared, that not even a child could place their fingertip on a portion of undamaged flesh.

"This must have been where it started. Where your soulless heart found and outlet for everything vile that is inside you. Hurling that whip; watching it lance her flesh filled your veins with adrenaline. Any sane person would have been frightened, ashamed and horrified that they were capable of such evil. But like a junkie that returns for another fix, you met her pleas for mercy with more flogging. You would wield that stick so fiercely that it knocked her to the ground. As she shrank from reach, writhing in pain, you raised it again. This is where you traded your soul for profane intoxication.

"I do not have words for her feet. I do not know how she put on shoes or walked. Swollen and blistered, open wounds that are saturated daily with bleach, shoved into shoes smaller than her size with nothing more than a threadbare sock for protection. And this festering quarter size open blister. I do not know how you sleep at night."

I surveyed the table covered with forty photographs.

I pictured the infamous scene in the 1992 movie, "A Few Good Men". Lt. Daniel Kaffee, played by Tom Cruise, is pounding Col. Nathan Jessup, played by Jack Nicholson, with questions, and he takes the bait. In a climatic twist, Col. Jessup erupts in a pompous tirade not only admitting, but boasting that he ordered the 'Code Red' that led to the death of a young marine.

Mrs. Hunter was equally as arrogant as the character, Col. Jessup. Her eyes steely pits of darkness where angels feared to tread. She was unremorseful and unashamed of the evidence sprawled across the table. Evidence that would assault anyone with a shred of human decency.

"Mrs. Hunter, you are not a mother trying her best to raise a child with a challenging past. You feel entitled and perversely gratified by your barbaric behavior. You systematically created an environment of castigating and pummeling two adopted children into submission. You dehumanized small children and methodically defiled every inch of Shantay's flesh like an animal marking their territory. Shantay's life holds no value in your eyes; she was a trophy of conquest. Your excuses are ludicrous, yet the ability to elude capture only intensified your delusion of grandeur. Without intervention your unhinged temper would have caused Shantay to suffer a traumatic brain injury or death.

"Adopting Anita and Shantay was a nefarious ruse to capture children and slowly devour them. You did not want the girls, but you took them in and treated them like subhuman property. Seething with resentment you immediately began taking it out on them. But no amount of abuse could quell the bitterness that consumed you. Tormenting became an elixir, but the satisfaction was transitory. Desperate to quench your masochistic thirst, you began contriving insidious new ways to brutalize Shantay emotionally, mentally, and physically. You withheld affection, safety, and comfort. You denied her access to her sister, recreation, music, art, friends, and a grade level education. In fact, when her teachers reported academic and behavioral successes, you punished her.

"You starved, over medicated, poisoned her and sentenced her to daily forced labor in hazardous and toxic conditions. Countless nights you banished Shantay to a concrete bed, cold, over medicated, faint from hunger, dehydrated, bleeding, throbbing in pain, and told to use a bucket for a toilet in the dark. Have I missed anything? Do not answer that. Mrs. Hunter, you have told so many lies, you lost track. You started taking risks, flaunting your conquests by sending her to school with untreated traumatic injuries. You thought you were invincible, but here you are. Look around. You are surrounded by bricks behind a locked door. Outside the door are men and women with weapons. I hope you feel it closing in because this, this is the future that awaits.

"Mrs. Hunter, you are under arrest for seven counts of malicious wounding, one count of administering a caustic substance, one count of replacing a medication with a poison, and an additional malicious wounding on behalf of your former adopted daughter, Anita for the abuse that resulted in her traumatic brain injury three years ago."

CHAPTER 30

Once Mrs. Hunter was taken to lock up, it was time to confront the man who branded Shantay with a scorching light bulb. The man who forfeited all parental responsibility and personified the worst possible example of fatherhood. The man who refused to protect the innocent. The man who tolerated and participated in the ritualistic dehumanization of two adopted girls. The man who cowardly abdicated his primary role as seven impressionable boys looked on. This would be our first and only conversation.

Mrs. Hunter was the primary abuser, but Mr. Hunter had experimented with his own techniques of torture. Burning Shantay with the light bulb. was particularly disturbing. He physically restrained Shantay and forced her eye open as his wife wickedly administered drops of poison into her eyes. He was as culpable as his wife. If he had a soul, remorse will compel him to unburden himself of guilt for his willful collusion.

Unfortunately, it is not a crime to be a passive husband married to a barbarian. He was aware of the abuse; he had seen the scars. There was no denying that. She had been forced to clean the bathroom in her underwear. Mrs. Hunter never attempted to hide the abuse or refrain from abusing openly. Every act of violence had been witnessed by others in view or nearby.

The only incident Shantay could recall where Mr. Hunter voiced his disapproval was in protest to the effects caused by Mrs. Hunter mixing bleach with ammonia. Even then, his objection was the fumes intruding on his personal comfort and not concern for her. Shantay was behind the closed bathroom door stepping in it and inhaling it. In the hours Shantay and I spoke, she never mentioned Mr. Hunter intervening.

I read Mr. Hunter his Miranda rights and he signed the form. Unlike his wife, he did not object to answering my questions. His responses were vague, and noncommittal. It was unclear whether he fully comprehended the questions. He was extremely nervous, squirming and frequently rubbing the back of his neck. Unlike his stiff-backed wife, he slouched and avoided eye contact. He seemed incapable of answering simple yes or no questions. My impression was that of a man who was browbeaten, and more fearful of repercussions from his wife than the law.

I began by asking about the dishes Shantay is forced to use; a single plastic plate, bowl, and spoon, and her being forbidden to touch any dishes other family members use. Initially he lied. When I drilled deeper, confronting him with evidence including his sons acknowledging that fact, he conceded. He claimed to believe she has a disease.

When asked about the weapons used to thrash, whip, and pummel Shantay, he spouted the default storyline used by his wife. The child constantly hurts herself. When I pressed in and asked specifically about the stick, playing on the "seed" that CPS planted indicating we found blood on it, he suddenly remembered seeing her in the backyard hitting herself. When I asked why he did not intervene and stop her. He was quiet for several minutes before saying it took him ten minutes to react. He could not think of a reason it took him ten minutes to walk outside when he saw her hitting herself. He could not recall why the stick was kept under the couch and not disposed of, or that tape was wrapped around one end of the stick because Mrs. Hunter got a splinter from it when beating Shantay. He reported watching her all the time but only seeing her hit herself once. He had no idea how the other scars, lacerations, bruises, and burns occurred. He insisted she was never hit with a stick or a switch. He denied burning her with a light bulb. or putting anything in her eye drops.

He insisted that he had been concerned about the wounds on Shantay's body but claimed he never saw how they were caused. He brought up her taking too many meds and having to constantly watch over her so she would not hurt herself. He could not explain why medications were sitting out if he and Mrs. Hunter were concerned about Shantay sneaking more than the dosage. He insisted it only took a split second for her to steal meds, which did not explain why they had not secured them for her safety.

Mr. Hunter acknowledged that Shantay cleaned the bathroom with bleach each day and that she did so without a shirt or pants to avoid bleach stains. He reluctantly admitted seeing her without clothes but initially stated he had not noticed she looked thin. Later when he was in the holding cell, he admitted that he knew she looked too thin. He was not concerned enough, by wounds too numerous to count, to question how they were inflicted, or to protect her or to seek professional help.

Mr. Hunter stated that Shantay's eye looks grey and cloudy because she has a disease. He told me it was not herpes, but he did not remember what the eye doctor called it; "something that begins with 'Hy'."

When I asked him about the injury to Shantay's lip, his story shifted. First, he acknowledged remembering when it happened. Then he recanted saying he had no idea how she got hurt. Later in the conversation, he remembered taking her to the doctor but did not know what caused the injury.

If Mr. Hunter was alarmed by the initial or accelerating abuse, he acquiesced, both tolerating and partaking in it. He could have defended Shantay, drawing the line after Anita's traumatic brain injury. But the abuse never subsided, it simply shifted to Shantay and intensified. Mr. Hunter could have advocated, in fact insisted that she be properly fed. Instead, like a coward, he complied. Indifferent to their suffering, he consented to the ruthless thrashings and the slow and deliberate vanquishing of their lives. His indifference was staggering.

Perhaps having the girls to brutalize redirected her hostility away from him and onto them. Whatever his excuse was, he was negligent, complicit, and I wanted to hold him accountable. Unfortunately, there were only two charges I could bring against him.

"Mr. Hunter, you are under arrest and being charged with one count of malicious wounding for burning Shantay with the light bulb., and one count of mixing poison in her medication."

~

Mr. and Mrs. Hunter were brought before the magistrate separately and processed to detainment. A bond hearing was set for the following day with the court granting a $250,000 bond for Mrs. Hunter. A preliminary hearing was set for General District Court six weeks later.

I was proud of the work and satisfied with the quality and strength of evidence. There was comfort in the knowledge that Shantay was safe and would never return to the Hunters. Such moments of victory are short lived, curbed by the legal system. Final disposition can take a year or longer. Anticipating their adjudication was bittersweet. Imagining the court condemning them for their crimes, and pronouncing swift judgement brought little consolation this evening. Prolonged litigation tends to favor the defendants. Time and familiarity anesthetize those nearest to the litigation process. The gravity of the violence and abuse blend into a sea of criminal activity and offenses. While lives hang in the balance, lawyers negotiate deals that further scourge victims. Justice would be deferred until a faraway date in the future.

CHAPTER 31

The journey from arrest to conviction was an excursive process. With a mountain of evidence to support the charges I was confident that justice would be served. I entered the waiting process continuing to take on cases and carrying them through the various stages of the litigation process. On average, I worked ninety-two cases each year, integrating two new cases into my workload most weeks.

Felony charges are presented in General District Court to ensure probable cause before moving forward to the grand jury and circuit court. The grand jury serves as another step in the process of ensuring sufficient evidence. The intense days following my introduction to Shantay at school, and culminating with their interrogations at headquarters, we accrued considerable substantiating evidence. Within a week my original incident report stretched to eighteen pages, even as I streamlined the facts we had accrued. Details encompassed both interviews with Shantay, evidence seized during the home search, findings obtained during by the trauma specialist's exam of Shantay at the hospital, dozens of photographs, information provided by school records and the prior contact with CPS and law enforcement and a 9-1-1 call.

It was five months before the grand jury was presented evidence that was received from the Division of Forensic Science Lab of Virginia confirming the contents of the "Refresh" tear bottle were ammonia. The lab further confirmed the presence of urine in the white bucket, and DNA testing confirmed the presence of blood on the mat was Shantay's.

After presenting the evidence to the grand jury, a true bill (indictment) was immediately handed down, and a warrant for the arrest of Mr. and Mrs. Hunter was issued. Both adoptive parents served several weeks in jail before bond was posted pending trial. Seven months following the Grand Jury Indictments, and twelve months following the intense first week of the investigation, the Hunter's entered into a plea agreement. Of the ten charges originally filed against Mrs. Hunter, she pled guilty to one count of "Child Abuse and Neglect", two counts of "Malicious Wounding", one for injuries inflicted on Shantay's sister Anita, and one count of "Adulteration of Food and Drink," and the other charges were formally dismissed, "Nolle Prosequi." Of the five charges filed against Mr. Hunter, he pled guilty to one count of "Child Abuse and Neglect," and one count of "Adulteration of Food and Drink," with the other charges formally dismissed, "Nolle Prosequi." Final disposition, sentencing was set for two and a half months later.

The apex of the arduous and convoluted legal mechanism, the day of reckoning and recompense finally arrived. I was anxious for the outcome and entered the courtroom early. Another case was being heard so I sat in the back of the courtroom to observe.

The case being heard was a felony uttering charge, first offense. The defendant seemed restless and annoyed. Following deliberations, the judge, incensed by the defendant's cavalier attitude, launched into a diatribe. He sentenced the defendant to ten years, suspending seven, ordering deputies to take him into custody. With a jolting thwack of his gavel, court was adjourned. The stunned defendant was escorted to detainment to begin his three-year sentence.

After a ten-minute recess, the court would sentence Mr. Hunter followed by Mrs. Hunter. I was appropriately optimistic. I hoped the judge's zeal for accountability would extend to Shantay's adoptive parents. Mrs. Hunter was incapable of curtailing her belligerence. If the court avenged the innocent with a penalty proportionate to the crime, this would indeed be a banner day.

The silence was deafening as the court flipped through the pages of the pre-sentencing report and recommendations. He appeared to be glancing as if nothing it contained would sway the conclusions he landed on. To my consternation, he took less time to contemplate his ruling than he had for the uttering charge in the previous case. In a devastating blow and disavowing the evidence he chose to empathize with the parents. In a stunning dereliction of duties, he stated he understood how challenging it can be when children antagonize their parents; that it can take them to the brink and cause them to lose it.

His reprehensible interpretation of the facts assailed me. His blatant disregard for the facts undermined the justice that made all our efforts worthwhile. He used this pivotal moment and his position of authority to passively pardon years of merciless abuse. The irrevocable damage they caused Shantay and Anita deserved less punishment than a bad check charge. I was bewildered. Diligent and thorough work seemingly invalidated. I was livid. To that point I had never felt such disrespect for a judge. He was not merely sympathizing, he empathized, and let them off the hook.

Throughout the hearing Mrs. Hunter was stoic and disengaged. Her face stern, her eyes cold as stone reflecting no contrition. In the end, the judge convicted Mrs. Hunter of two counts of Malicious Wounding, one for the abuse that led to Anita's traumatic brain injury, one for Child Abuse and Neglect, and one for Adulteration of Food/Drink. The sentences would run concurrently, and the court suspended all but one year in prison for the first three charges and all but three years in prison for the fourth. Mrs. Hunter would serve a maximum of three years. Twice in my twenty-five-year law enforcement career have I seen a defendant physically restrained after sentencing. Mrs. Hunter was the first. When she finally understood she would serve jail time, she erupted in rage and hysteria. I have never witnessed such undignified, unbridled mania in the courtroom. She threw herself on the floor cursing flailing her body like she was having a seizure. Deputies attempted to restrain her, but her combativeness escalated. As deputies approached her, she thrashed her arms and kicked like a maniac. I half-expected them to use their stun gun. When they finally secured her in handcuffs and shackles, she refused to stand. Unable to lift dead weight, several deputies had to drag her by the ankles.

I wondered if the judge regretted his decision. As gratifying as it was to watch her true colors so humiliatingly displayed, it did not quell my indignation. What was the judge thinking? I hope to heaven Shantay never knows this happened. Another system failed her. God, how could you allow them to get away with this? Where is your justice? The ruling was a powerful uppercut to my confidence. There was no room for ambiguity in the exhaustive evidence. No cause to doubt. When did the application of every moral and legal tenet become subjective? Disillusionment almost took me out, and I began to question if it was time to turn in my badge. Despite that and other devastating setbacks I remained in the fight. My commitment to children and my dedication to the Crimes Against Children Taskforce lasted three more years. The Hunters were released from prison before I retired.

~

As stated previously, I remained in touch with Shantay and her new family. I celebrated her continued growth and maturation in the loving environment provided by her foster mother. Michaela adopted Shantay and her other foster daughter, and they became a family. I attended various celebrations and watched her blossom hope against hope.

She immediately began to thrive academically, and her grades soared. I researched and found a local doctor able to repair the damage to her earlobes. By sixth grade she was donning pierced earrings again. In a handwritten note thanking me for fixing her ears, she proudly shared that she had achieved honor roll and won first place among sixth graders during an oral presentation.

Shantay's progress became a beacon in the darkness, the outcome I desired for every case I worked. Watching her life continually expand and be restored had enriched my own. Her strength and resilience inspired me. Within a few years of settling into her last and permanent family, she seemed to overcome the odds in an extraordinary way. She proved many wrong. When I found myself discouraged, her story was the one that helped me remain vigilant to the cause.

During high school I set out on a quest to find a doctor to replace her severely damaged eye with a prosthetic eye. The process took time and patience, but the results were transformative. Her appearance and comfort level improved dramatically. Her self-confidence soared as she prepared to launch into the world.

By senior year, many of the prominent scars had faded. Only a few deep grooves remained. Her skin was otherwise flawless. A radiant smile and adorable dimples appeared where only trepidation and rejection shone through years before. If you placed her senior photo next to her fifth-grade photo you would not believe they were the same girl. I wondered if the Hunters would even recognize the beautiful young woman she had become.

The first time Shantay told me she had dreams of one day being strong enough to tell her story, was in junior high. I do not recall how the topic turned in that direction. She may have heard someone at the Christian school or at church share their testimony. I always believed that she should. We had a similar conversation a few years later as she shared her intended field of study for college. I was struck by the deep well of courage she summoned to look me in the eye and say, "Someday I will find a way to be a voice for the voiceless."

Like all teenagers she was influenced by social media and the pressure to conform. Family could not slake the desire for the acceptance of peers. Eager to belong, longing to be invited, hoping to be chosen for the team, included with the popular kids, asked out by the one you are crushing on.

The transition between teenager and young adult is frequently a tempestuous journey. The clash between Shantay and her mom erupted like a hair trigger. Neither mom or daughter could identify what was unraveling or why.

Shantay felt conflicted. From the time she entered Michaela's home she had been immensely grateful for the ways her life had been transformed. Ordinary pleasures felt lavish, and she received them with childlike wonder. She never forgot that life had given her another chance through Michaela. She felt rescued from nightmares other children were still experiencing, maybe even in her newer middle-class neighborhood. When she perceived her mother did not trust her, she felt ashamed and unworthy.

Shantay's psyche was not as developed, or healed, as her age and appearance. Vital stages in her early development were impeded by ten years of living hell. The wake rippled for years. When her inner and outer worlds began to collide, she had no language to articulate the turmoil. Her mother could not see that strict protection triggered feeling controlled and denied what others had. A storm of resentment was building. Both mom and daughter were driven by fear. Mom's fear caused her to tighten her grip. Shantay's fear caused her to resist and flee.

She envied other girls being allowed to date and have boys over. The unhealed messages from early childhood usurped the years of trust they had built. Her mother's protection translated as controlling punishment. Mistrust drove a wedge between their sweet and fun-loving relationship. Shantay was counting down to independence and free agency to decide "good and bad" for herself.

I supposed some might wonder if Kevin, her college sweetheart turned violent abuser and murderer, was a victim of childhood abuse. Did he watch his dad beat his mom? Was he repeating a generational cycle. I am inclined to believe he was just a bully, an immature, ill-tempered and insecure boy, who exploited a young woman to feel better about himself.

CHAPTER 32

The bereaved waiting in line at the funeral home were growing restless. Many others grieving, weeping, and wanting to offer Michaela their condolences. I needed to withdraw from the intensity of the conversation. I wanted to rejoin my wife. The person behind me took the pause between us as a cue and approached Michaela. As she turned to acknowledge them, I stepped away.

I glanced at Becky sitting on a loveseat in the corner. She was intently listening to another guest and appeared to be consoling them. I walked to the opposite corner where Michaela's mother Lori was sitting with Anna. Anna was playing quietly with a doll.

"Hello Lori, I am heartbroken for you and your family. I cannot believe Shantay is gone. Such a beautiful young woman. Then I knelt next to Anna and waited for her to look up. Anna, I knew your momma when she was a little girl. She was beautiful just like you are. She was special to me, and I loved her very much. You made her happier than anything else in the world. I hope someday we meet again," I said to her softly.

"Thank you," she said nodding.

I returned to Becky, so grateful for her presence. We walked toward the screen looping a pictorial slide show. The photos began when Shantay entered Michaela's life. There were a handful of Shantay with Anita when they visited her in the group home. Anita's health continued to decline until she died of complications from her injuries. The last photos of the girls together, Anita was unconscious. We watched as the photos told a narrative of a transformed life. Most people in the room knew little or nothing about her life before Michaela. There she was, our brave Leo the Lion girl, smiling like a champion who had, against all odds, overcome the worst abuse case I had worked. As she grew in stature and the love of her family, her face showed less of the burden she carried the first ten years. Photos documented a girl growing and enjoying a life she and others never dreamed possible. Countless photos captured her beautiful smile and spontaneous laughter, testifying to the love she found with a real family, and how much her life had been redeemed.

Michaela had opened her arms and scarcity was gone. Shantay's life was filled with tutus and hopscotch, chorus, and speeches. There were birthday parties, Easter baskets, and sandcastles by the shore. Photos of Thanksgiving and Christmas showed the girls surrounded by extended family. There were pictures of her with her adopted sister and their friends' and other classmates. There were celebratory events including her baptism, and the girls at their junior high and senior high graduations.

I was grateful that they included a few of her and I together. One was at her high school graduation, the last time I saw her. Shantay and her sister graduated the same year, both wearing white dresses for the ceremony at the Christian school. Shantay's legs withstood the worst of Mrs. Hunter's wrath and many scars had not faded. It made her self-conscious and she covered them with stockings. Shantay wore a purple sash for receiving an advanced diploma in biology and maintaining honor roll. What the smaller school lacked in quantity of students it made up for in devotion to the students and quality education. Each graduate was spotlighted, and faculty members took turns honoring their individual and team accomplishments including scholarships awarded for college.

During the reception that followed, I hugged Shantay and congratulated her. I told her how proud I was of her hard work and reminded her how bright and hopeful her future was. She and Michaela led me to family members I had not met, once again introducing me as "her hero." With appetizers in hand, Shantay and I stepped away from the crowd for a few minutes and sat together. I handed her a card with a gift inside. She took her time reading my words and thanked me for all I had done. How do you explain that no thanks were needed? It was not just my job, it was all that life had prepared me to be part of. I counted myself fortunate and honored to have been in her life to observe her transformation. We talked again about sharing her story. She hoped to one day find the words, but that would have to wait until after college.

The nostalgia of our last conversation on the day of her graduation flooded in. I felt extraordinarily blessed to have known her and to see her miraculous transformation. The bittersweetness of it all. Our best efforts had not saved her in the end, and it was excruciating. I console myself in knowing and witnessing the best years.

The most recent photos were of Shantay and Anna. Her countenance reflected a different joy than the other photos. Despite it being an unplanned pregnancy that sidetracked her academic goals, she delighted in Anna. There is something redemptive about a newborn that creates bridges between estranged family members. Babies usher us quicker to reconciliation than time and distance ever will. That was true for Michaela and Shantay. They returned to a circle of trust, one that supplied shelter and support for Shantay in times of vulnerability and need.

My heart sank when the loop of photographs started over and I realized how few captured Shantay with Michaela. It was in thousands of tireless undocumented moments that Shantay's life had been rebuilt. Only a few of those were caught on film. Now those moments were committed to Michaela's memories, and to the memories of those who were fortunate enough to know and love her.

Before we left the memorial service, I pulled Michaela aside to say goodbye. I reminded her that the legal process can be a long and grueling journey. It will take time and she will need patient endurance. I assured her the detectives would work diligently to find

Kevin and for justice to be served. No matter how long it takes, when the day comes, I promised to join her in the courtroom.

I do not remember much about the drive home from the memorial service. Just a few hours earlier we had seen sunlight burning through the clouds like a message from heaven. Now it was dark and bitter cold. I was encouraged by the crowd of people that attended. So many people supporting Michaela and her family. Anna is adorable and Shantay would live on through her sweet daughter. This was not an ending anyone could have imagined. I had once envisioned myself at her wedding. She would introduce me to the man she loved, one who was worthy of her trust and saw the beautiful soul we saw. It was never to be.

CHAPTER 33

For five weeks the man who murdered Shantay eluded capture. The manhunt spanned several states. Police continued to implore citizens to report any information regarding his whereabouts.

As details began to emerge, we learned that Kevin called her cell phone at 7:03 a.m. the morning of the murder. Cell phone tower pings verified the call ended at 7:10 a.m. near her apartment. Shockingly, he was captured on surveillance video at a nearby convenience store at 7:25 a.m. where he was seen withdrawing cash from the ATM. He fled south to a relative's home asking to borrow money, then continued south.

As the crime scene was examined, evidence revealed that he used the upstairs bathroom to clean up. Traces of blood were found on the towels; bloody handprints were found on the floor and smeared blood on the sliding glass door. Police also found broken fingernails. A business card with contact information for the police officer that helped her obtain the restraining order was found in Shantay's purse,

Detectives monitored Kevin's cell phone for activity and contacted law enforcement agencies in localities he traveled through. U.S. Marshall's joined the multi-state manhunt homing in on the fugitive with a first-degree murder warrant. Local crime solvers continued asking the community to report any information about the crime or Kevin's possible whereabouts.

Several weeks into the search Kevin contacted another relative who confronted him about the murder while recording the conversation. During the call Kevin apologized for hurting everybody and said he did not know what had happened; only that they had been arguing, he walked past the kitchen but was not aware that he had a knife in his hand. He then claimed to have swallowed pills with the intention of killing himself. He called 9-1-1 then hung up, eventually emerging from a wooded area where he had been hiding out, suffering from an overdose.

As the wheels of justice slowly turned, and seven months after his extradition back to Virginia, the evidence was presented to the grand jury. Without hesitation they certified a true bill for first degree murder. The case was set for a jury trial.

Two weeks before Kevin was scheduled to face a jury of his peers, he entered into a plea agreement with an amended charge of 2nd degree murder, reduced based on lack of premeditation.

During the plea hearing, a photograph of Shantay's bloody body surrounded by a pool of blood was presented. The grisly details of the autopsy report were disclosed. The medical examiners indicated there were defensive wounds including broken fingernails and a cut on her finger. They concluded that the first knife wound caused a superficial injury, but the second knife wound was catastrophic. The 6-foot, 2-inch, 235-pound former defensive linebacker lunged upon her with brute strength thrusting the knife deeply into her chest, aiming for her heart. Blood coursed profusely, saturating her clothing, and pooling around her body as her life ebbed away. Kevin, fully cognizant of his actions, hurriedly washed his blood-stained hands and wiped away the blood spatter from his face, neck, arms and shirt. Shantay lay dying alone, in anguish and terror for several minutes. The medical examiner determined that her death resulted from bleeding out or when the cavity around her heart filled with blood and ceased pumping.

Sentencing would take place three months later, affording the prosecution and defense time to prepare their evidence to support opposing sentencing recommendations.

~

199

Thirteen years after meeting Shantay, and nine years after retiring from law enforcement, I returned to circuit court. The hallowed halls where justice hung by a thread and could slip from your fingers in an instant. The dreadful moment when Shantay's adoptive parents received hand-slaps for their atrocities poked accusingly at my heart. I could not bear another judicial travesty that reduced her life to a sad but statistically expected outcome.

I could not recall the last time I entered the courthouse as a civilian. It was strange waiting in line to pass through security. No badge, no county ID, no bypassing the magnetometer with a wave from the deputies. Peculiar how time moves on in our absence; continually changing but much the same.

I felt out of place and oddly vulnerable walking the long corridor I once frequented. No longer in the trenches, I was older, wiser, but still a wounded soldier in a throng of law enforcement veterans who had given their lives for a thousand unseen battles. Decades of expertise and camaraderie were now a faded memory. We volunteered to fight in this war; a war where heroes are no longer considered heroic. A sacrificial life where the media and the citizens now scrutinize every move. We swear an oath to serve and protect those hellbent on vilifying.

My favorite redemptive story had been thwarted in an inconceivably gruesome manner. Now the moment arrested me. The moment of recompense for the man who took her life rested in one person's hands. Years ago, one person had ruled her life was of such little value that he sanctioned the couple who tried to destroy her with a minimal sentence for their crimes. Rarely had I felt so powerless.

I remembered a similar feeling as I sat interviewing a ten-year-old girl a second time. We shared chocolate chip cookies and glasses of milk. She sat next to a Leo the Lion stuffed animal, a symbol of rare beauty and courage. She had poured her heart out and let me into a secret world that she had never disclosed to another. I had wanted to believe, more than any other time I could remember, that her life would be different. That light could indeed overcome the darkness. I cannot say during which moment I felt more helpless.

I thought about the brave little girl with knowledge of sorrow, pain and suffering no child should ever endure. I thought about the brave little girl who found courage larger than life to rise above her ravished childhood and turn her life around. I thought about the brave young woman, with a brilliant future, brimming with potential and possibility hijacked by the return of violence. I thought about the young woman, who found courage larger than life to break free and rise like a Phoenix from the ashes as I always imagined she would. I thought about the brave young woman who found courage larger than life to suffer alone as she lay dying.

Three hours had been allotted for the sentencing hearing. I verified the docket, relieved it was not in the same courtroom where the Hunters were sentenced.

Although we had spoken, I had not seen Michaela since the memorial service a year ago. Another holiday season would be eclipsed by death, and reminders of profound loss that will echo for years. Michaela was surrounded by people filling several rows near the front. I approached quietly and tapped her on the shoulder. I hugged her, and some family members and shook hands with friends from her church and friends of Shantay's there to testify. I had no capacity for chit-chat, and quickly turned forward and sat down. I could not shake the thoughts of the other judge's ruling.

As I scanned the courtroom my eyes fell on the Judge's nameplate. I had been so prepared for the worst; it took a moment to sink in. When it did, it took every modicum of self-control for me to maintain my composure. Oh, thank God! I wanted to stand up and shout aloud. This judge is tough, poised but intimidating. She is fair, but not to be trifled with. A judge with no tolerance for those who disrespect the law, the court, or the bench. I was elated. We had a chance for a just outcome.

The trial was long and emotionally intense, as the defense and prosecution lobbied. The defense had little to defend the evidence presented by the Commonwealth Attorney. Every element was poignant, sealing his fate. Victim impact statements, the protective order Shantay filed against Kevin six weeks prior to the murder and corresponding facts outlined in the police report. Photos of her memorial book were presented, and transcripts and screen shots of text messages were revealed.

Friends of Shantay testified that she had disclosed some of the defendant's history of violence against her. They recounted specific incidents including when he tried to push her out a window, and another time beating a male visitor of Shantay's in her home. They testified that he would take her phone away, isolating her and preventing friends and family from contacting her. He also intercepted and deleted communications.

Three individuals read their victim impact statements, including Michaela. It was heart wrenching. Michaela wore the purple sash Shantay wore during her high school graduation. She talked about adopting Shantay and how badly abused she had been by another family in the community. A family that had beaten, starved, and even forced her to live in the shed.

It was at that moment that the Judge looked at me. The wheels that had been turning below the surface suddenly clicked. She knew exactly why I was in the courtroom, with the family. Her eyes affirmed her understanding. I was the detective that worked her abuse case thirteen years ago.

Michaela shared Shantay's dream of becoming a counselor for at-risk youth and the classes she had enrolled in at the local community college. She shared firsthand knowledge of the incident a few weeks prior to the murder when he had choked Shantay to unconsciousness. You could have heard a pin drop as she described the terrifying events of finding her daughter's body. Arriving at the apartment, finding the door unlocked, repeatedly calling out her name, walking upstairs and seeing her baby lying on the floor, blood everywhere. She had no doubt then or now who was responsible, stating her daughter was violently taken away by the heinous act of a monster.

The prosecution's closing argument affirmed the defendant's lack of remorse over Shantay's death proving he clearly does not care about anyone other than himself.

In a desperate and unsuccessful attempt to extenuate his client's actions and circumvent the evidence, the defense suggested his client might suffer from chronic traumatic encephalopathy, a degenerative brain disease that has been found in football players who suffer repeated concussions. During questioning the defendant's mother testified that her son began playing football in middle school and sometimes would complain of head injuries.

Moments before the court would render its ruling, the defendant was asked if he had anything to say. Initially he was contrite offering the family this statement, "I'm sorry about the amount of pain and sadness I brought you."

The judge was unconvinced that Kevin had ever suffered a concussion, stating no evidence had been presented. After advising the defendant to stand, she looked him directly in the eye and said, "Your lack of remorse, your utter disregard for human life is apparent." He was sentenced to fifty years in prison with 10 years suspended, followed by fifty years of probation upon release.

For the second time in my twenty-five-year law enforcement career, I saw a defendant react when hearing their sentencing with a crazed outburst. He began cursing and railing against the judge and others in the courtroom. Deputies raced toward him tackling him to the ground, piling on top to restrain him before removing him from the courtroom.

There are no words to describe the relief I felt knowing her life had finally been vindicated. It was a bittersweet victory, but the outcome was much deserved. This case was one of many challenging and tragic cases. Shantay's story, and the life that followed her rescue were personally impactful. I had hoped that she would overcome and enjoy her life to the fullest. It broke my heart to learn that her life ended the way it began. There is no place to neatly tuck that away, and I never have.

Shantay's life was taken before she could tell her story and help others by doing so. Sharing her courageous story of child abuse, rescue and murder is denying evil the power to silence her voice and proves that light will always overcome the darkness.

EPILOGUE

Thank you for taking this journey with us. We know this was not an easy read. It is our heartfelt desire to leave readers with a sense of honor for the brave officers, social service workers, nurses, and doctors for often thankless work you do, and hope and help for anyone struggling in silence.

There are children waiting for someone to step into their lives and rescue them. "Victim" is not their identity, nor is it a life sentence. Victimization does not have the last word. If we do not believe that, how can they?

The battle is fierce, heart wrenching and can seem futile. These interventions have an unseen cost. The resources available for the unique types of post-traumatic stress experienced by first responders have increased exponentially in the last decade. We gathered much of the most current information and posted it to our website for you and your loved ones to utilize. www.brandedforlife.net.

The most encouraging news is a shift in the language confronting the stigma. There is an overdue recognition that post-traumatic stress is most often an injury and not a disorder (and perceived label for life). Injuries can heal. It may take time. It may require a lifestyle change. It will require engaging honestly with others. Please do not wait until you are in crisis. Be proactive about mental wellness. You are irreplaceable and your presence in this world invaluable.

"TRAUMA is our personal intersection with the brokenness of the world. RECOVERY is our personal intersection with the redemptive heart of God." www.RebootRecovery.com

You cannot give what you do not have. Take care of yourselves and each other. Build and sustain your reserve of resilience. Pursue healthy friendships with healthy individuals. Exploring new ways to expand the ways you turn from the darkness and toward the light; ways that recenter you. Nurturing mental health is more instinctive than we realize when we approach well-being holistically. Art, nature, music, laughter, spirituality, hiking, gardening, playing an instrument, biking, yoga, cooking, fishing, drawing, sports, writing, woodworking, solitude, pottery, kayaking, painting, meditation; the list is endless. Simple pleasures such watching a sunrise and sunset, standing near the ocean or a stream, bird watching, and star gazing can be extremely soothing.